THE
GREATEST
RAILROAD
STORY
EVER TOLD

THE GREATEST RAILROAD STORY EVER TOLD

*Henry Flagler & the Florida
East Coast Railway's Key West Extension*

SETH H. BRAMSON

THE
History
PRESS

Published by The History Press

Charleston, SC 29403

www.historypress.net

Copyright © 2011 by Seth H. Bramson

All rights reserved

All images are courtesy of the author unless otherwise noted.

First published 2011

ISBN 978-1-5402-0630-5

Library of Congress CIP data applied for.

Contents

He is, unquestionably and undoubtedly, "Our Founder," for with the exception of such as Henry Huntington in California or James J. Hill and Henry Villard in the Pacific Northwest, no one person has ever done as much to build an entire region as Henry Morrison Flagler (1830–1913). The single greatest name in the history of the Sunshine State, Flagler was, is and always will be known as Florida's "Empire Builder."

DEDICATION

This book must be doubly dedicated. First, to all those who are no longer with us but who played a part in the construction, maintenance and operation of the Key West Extension, a special salute, in memoriam, is long overdue and is given with unending gratitude for all they did those many years ago.

Second, this book must also be dedicated to Claudia Pennington, executive director, and David Harrison Wright, president of the board of directors of the Key West Art and Historical Society. It has been through their guidance and leadership that the society's museum at the Custom House in Key West has become one of America's finest. Additionally, it must also be noted that it was only through their foresight and perseverance that this book was commissioned in order to present to the American public, on the 100th anniversary of the arrival of Henry Flagler into Key West on the first passenger train, the greatest railroad story ever told. Gratefully, I, as author, quote a wise and beloved personage in saying to Claudia and David, not only "thank you," but also "live long and prosper."

ACKNOWLEDGEMENTS

U nlike all of my previous books, and with only one exception in this book, the listing of the groups and individuals who helped to make this book possible is, truly, one of those "Where do I start?" moments!

The one exception to that question is, of course, with our (now) dear and close friends at the Key West Art and Historical Society, owners and operators of the Custom House and its incredible Florida Keys history museum. Simply put, without executive director Claudia Pennington and president of the board of directors David Harrison Wright it is entirely possible that this book might not have been written, and my gratitude to them for their total support and complete faith in me is boundless.

Since we have to "start" somewhere now that the initial "thank you" has been written, the next statement of complete appreciation must be given to the beloved Jeane and Irving R. Eyster; their daughter, Barbara Edgar; Barbara's gentleman admirer, David Purdo; and Barbara's beautiful daughter, Cinnamon, who means so much and has been such an inspiration to us all.

Jeane and Irving founded the Matecumbe Historical Trust, and after years of dedication to the preservation of Florida Keys history, the beautiful Irving R. Eyster Museum of Florida Keys History, named in honor of Mr. Eyster, is scheduled to open with a grand ceremony on April 12, 2012. (The trust's website is www.matecumbehistoricaltrust.com.) Dr. Dan Gallagher can certainly not be overlooked. His tremendous research and writings on the extension have provided incredible amounts of information, and we are beyond grateful to Dan for all he has done to record the history of the Key West Extension.

Tom Hambright, longtime director of the Florida collection of the Monroe County Public Library in Key West has not only done a yeoman's job of preserving Florida Keys historic memorabilia but also was beyond gracious in loaning several rare images and providing information for this book available from no other known source.

Also in Key West, Ed Swift and Phyllis and Steve Strunk have been great advocates of Oversea Railway memorabilia preservation, and Ed's and Steve's contributions must be and are noted with great gratitude.

In Miami, Jonathan Nelson has, for many years, worked to preserve FEC memorabilia, while HistoryMiami, particularly Dawn Hughes in the reference and research center, has, for a good few years, warmly welcomed my requests for assistance and information. In West Palm Beach, the beloved Jim Ponce has spent innumerable years keeping the Flagler Hotels story alive.

Joan Langley and her dear husband, the late Wright Langley, spent many years preserving Keys history and the history of the railroad, and I want Joan to be aware of how appreciative all are who knew Wright and know her for everything they have done for the preservation of Keys history.

Calvin Winter, president of the FEC Railway Society, wrote a marvelous history of the car ferry service in the society's *Speedway* magazine, and I thank him for a great article, a good bit of which is quoted in the "Trumbo Island Terminal" chapter. I am also indebted to Mark Poormon for furnishing the great photo of mile post marker KW 275/JAX 247, which has a place of honor on display in his home, as well as to Jerry Groothouse of Fort Pierce, who so graciously provided the September 5, 1935 view of the injured veterans who survived the storm being tended to next to a freight car.

Special thanks must also be extended to Max Imberman, who, while interning with me during the summer of 2011, assisted greatly in filing and cataloguing much of "the stuff."

The thank yous would not be complete without a word of great appreciation to our IT director and webmaster, Adam Rogers, who has once again come through like the champ he is.

Finally—and it does not "go without saying" but rather *needs* to be said—none of this could have been done without the complete support of my bride. A mere thank you in showing my appreciation for Myrna's forbearance and tolerance as I laid "stuff" out all over the house in preparation for the writing of this book is simply not enough to tell her that I "couldn't a done it without you!"

While it is, at this juncture, important for me to state that, in several cases, requests for input or information were either ignored or overlooked, nobody who helped, volunteered to help or tried to help was intentionally "left out," but if I did not mention one or more individuals who contributed thoughts, ideas, information or memorabilia, they have my sincere apologies, as well as assurances that their involvement will be included in future editions.

Introduction

This book is a story of superlatives. Henry Morrison Flagler—Florida's "Empire Builder"—was, is and always will be the single greatest name in the history of Florida, while the Key West Extension of the Flagler-owned Florida East Coast Railway was, is and will always remain—absolutely, positively, unequivocally, inarguably and incontestably—the greatest railroad engineering and construction feat in U.S. (and, possibly, world) history.

The building of that railroad was not just a matter of *how* but also, and more importantly, of *when*. Almost everything the builders of the railroad did was a first—in engineering, in construction and in the art and discipline of American railroad building.

There are those individuals (probably the same people who still believe the fable known in South Florida as "the orange blossom myth"—that Mr. Flagler extended his railroad to the shores of Biscayne Bay because Julia Tuttle, one of Miami's early pioneers, supposedly sent him some orange blossoms following the great Florida freezes of December 1894 and January and February 1895) who have had, through the years, the temerity to refer to the Key West Extension as "Flagler's Folly," a charge and comment that was and is pure, unadulterated hooey.

Although the first article propounding a railroad to Key West appeared in print (according to Sidney Walter Martin on page 202 of *Florida's Flagler*) as early as 1831 (Mr. Flagler then only one year old), with another article following in another Key West paper four years later, and although famed Confederate general John B. Gordon (one of the numerous high-ranking former Confederate officers who, once the Civil War ended, strongly supported full restoration of the Union) incorporated and chartered the Great Southern Railroad in Florida in 1870 with the right to build numerous lines within the state, including one to Key West, and even with the *National Geographic* magazine article written by Key West's famed collector of customs Jefferson B. Browne in 1896 propounding the building of a railroad through the Florida Keys with Key West as its terminal, Key West—at the time the article was written, Florida's largest city—was not Flagler's initial destination of choice.

The railroad's terminal would, of course, eventually be Key West, and it would be the railroad's extension to the island city that would cement Flagler's fame and legend for all time. But this book is not simply a story of an incredible construction feat; rather, it tells of the life and times of the operation of a great railroad, how it was managed, who rode it, what it did for the Florida Keys and what it meant to the conchs, the residents of the Keys and Key West.

In addition to the railroad, though, Flagler and the railroad's (and the hotel company's) subsequent managers understood that there had to be ancillary services to make people recognize the usefulness, viability and need to patronize the railroad and its affiliates. Hence, there were the hotels, the Key West Terminal and the FEC Car Ferry Company, with its daily round trips to Cuba, carrying vital railroad car loads of freight to and from Key West en route to and from the rest of America. In addition, the Flagler System–owned Peninsular & Occidental Steamship Company provided regular passenger service from Knight's Key to Havana (1908–12) and from Key West to Havana thereafter, and all of that is part of this incredible story.

The reader may be aware that there have been several books written on or about the Key West Extension, but except for the very first one, Pat Parks's original 1968 *The Railroad that Died at Sea*—which, although giving a brief history of the line, focused on the construction and on the terrible Labor Day 1935 hurricane that ended service on the Keys segment of the railroad— the others have either dealt almost exclusively with the construction and engineering challenges of building the railroad that went to sea (Dr. Dan Gallagher's heavily researched *Florida's Great Ocean Railway* the single finest example of that genre) or on the September 2, 1935 storm, which swept away more than forty miles of roadbed and right of way, destroyed the Long Key Fishing Camp and killed more than eight hundred people. Those books, of which there have been several, also discussed, to relatively limited extents, the aftermath of the storm.

This book, then, is a first: it is the first book written on that great project that will not only explain how and why the route to Key West was chosen and who the important figures were during the railroad's construction, but it will also examine and discuss the daily operation of the railway and how it was maintained, the reason for opening the Long Key Fishing Camp (the Flagler System's only casual inn or resort) and the later (1918–20) construction by the hotel company of the Casa Marina at Key West.

The chapters include, for the first time in print, photos of many of the stations, rights of way and, of course, the bridges, as well as views in, of and at the Trumbo Island, Key West terminal, in effect bringing the operation of this great railroad to life.

Although discussing the 1935 hurricane (with photos never before published, including the only known views of the train that was caught in the storm at Matecumbe *after* it had been brought back to Miami's Buena Vista Yard), the book concludes not only with a look at the conversion of the right of way to the over-the-sea highway following that storm but also with a chapter devoted to the memory of the great project and to those who have worked so hard and for so long to ensure that what was done to connect the Keys to the mainland between 1904 and 1912 will never be forgotten. Hence, tribute is warmly paid, as the finale of the book, to, among others, Claudia Pennington, director of the Key West Art & Historical Society and board of directors president David Harrison Wright and their colleagues for the magnificent exhibit at the Custom House in Key West that will forever memorialize the great task, as well as for being sponsors of this book. Tribute is also paid to historians Joan and the late Wright Langley, Jeane and Irving Eyster and the Matecumbe Historical Trust (which they founded); Dr. Dan Gallagher, whose research efforts and marvelously informative books have preserved and maintained so much in photographs and information; and Ed Swift and Steve Strunk, who have done so much to preserve the memories of the extension, as well as others who have played a role in preservation.

Come now and enjoy your ride on the over-the-sea railway, but do be sure, en route, to tarry long enough to join me for lunch at Long Key Fishing Camp and relish the freshly caught broiled pompano, the key lime pie and the iced coffee. And while we are there in the dining room at the main lodge, enjoying a nonpareil view of the Atlantic, perhaps Zane Grey will stop at our table to visit with us and chat. In any event, please take your coach or parlor car seat, or settle back in your Pullman sleeping car room, and relive with me the greatest railroad story ever told.

1

IN THE BEGINNING

While this book is not meant to be a biography of Henry Morrison Flagler, an overview for the purpose of gaining an understanding of who he was and why he did what he did is certainly in order. Hence, a brief retrospective of a man whose legacy is that of the single greatest person in the history of the Sunshine State is, at this juncture, quite apropos.

In effect, the story is similar to a biblical parable, for Henry Flagler looked at Florida shortly after his arrival and said, "This is good." And then he said, "Let there be hotels," and lo, there were hotels. And then he said, "Let there be railroads," and lo, there were railroads. And then he said, "Let there be land companies, and cities, and newspapers, and water and gas and electric companies, and paved streets and bridges," and lo, there were all of those things. Henry Flagler looked at what he had done in Florida and said, "This is good," and if one were to encapsulate the work of Mr. Flagler, that is *it*. But without fleshing out the story, there might be a lack of understanding as to the "why" and the "how," and that is the purpose of this chapter, for, simply put, Henry Flagler never "rested." Instead, he simply moved from great project to great project and, in the course of that work and those projects, became nothing less than a true legend in Florida's history.

Regretfully, no small amount of what has been written on and about Flagler is either completely wrong, riddled with errors or sadly and woefully

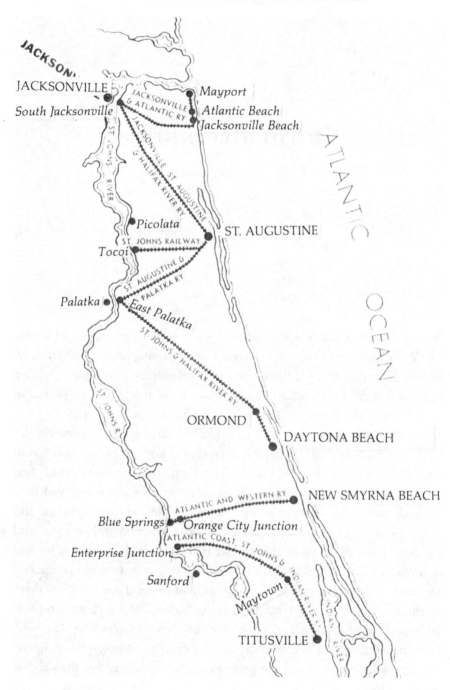

Railroads on the upper east coast of Florida prior to Mr. Flagler's purchase and construction efforts to consolidate them (and others, not shown) into what would, in 1895, become the Florida East Coast Railway.

In the Beginning

On December 31, 1885, Henry Flagler purchased the Jacksonville, St. Augustine & Halifax River Railroad, at the time a rickety little narrow-gauge line that connected the south bank of the St. Johns River with St. Augustine. That was his first railroad endeavor, and he bought the railroad only so that he could expedite the flow of construction materiel to the site of the hotels he was building in the ancient city. Here, five employees of the railroad are shown with 4-4-0 number two, the W. Jerome Green Jr.

inadequate or misstated. The single best source for information on his life remains the first biography of him ever written, by Sidney Walter Martin, originally published in 1952 by the University of Georgia Press and titled *Florida's Flagler*. Subsequent biographies offered little new information, likely, to no small extent, because the authors were either unaware of or chose not to avail themselves of the railway company's archives, located in Miami. Those archives contain an immense amount of unpublished material on and about Mr. Flagler and his and the Flagler System's great works. For the first time, in this book, those archives will be fully taken advantage of. That being stated, Dr. Martin's book remains the preeminent source for previously published biographical material on Flagler.

Henry Flagler was born on January 2, 1830, in the little village of Hopewell, in upstate New York, to Elizabeth and Isaac Flagler. Both Elizabeth and Isaac had been married twice before, and Henry had a half-sister (his father's daughter from a previous marriage) named Ann-Caroline, or "Carrie," and a half-brother, Dan Harkness (his mother's son from her second marriage, to David Harkness, who died in 1825).

Until Mr. Flagler built the first bridge spanning the St. Johns River, all traffic had to cross by ferry, the Jacksonville, St. Augustine & Halifax River Railway's "Armsmear" shown here.

The Harkness family was from Ohio, and although Dan lived with his mother and stepfather, he, being eight years older than Henry, left New York in 1837 to return to Ohio to work in the retail businesses his late father had founded. Fortunately, even with the age difference, Dan and Henry developed a great fondness for each other.

Henry's father was an itinerant Presbyterian minister and moved frequently from one impoverished congregation to another, but once Dan had left New York to return to Ohio, Henry, anxious to remove himself from what, to him, was a burdensome and always penurious existence, made up his mind that, at some point, he would follow in Dan's footsteps.

According to several Internet sources, Flagler's parents separated in 1838, but there is no mention of that occurrence in Martin's book, and indeed, upon Henry's departure from the family home in New York in 1844 to join Dan in Ohio, Martin notes that "he gave his parents a fond farewell then turned slowly and started down the little path leading from the house." This seems to indicate that, if his parents had, at some point, separated, they were, by the time of Henry's setting out in the world for himself, back together.

After an arduous journey by foot, buckboard, canal boat and lake steamer, Henry arrived in Republic, Ohio, where he was met by Dan and put to work at a general store owned by Dan's uncle. As difficult as it is to believe today, the young Flagler was paid $5 a month, plus room and board. Dan managed the store for his uncle, and Henry worked exceedingly hard for his half-brother. Sparing the reader the excruciating details, Henry would eventually be moved to the Harkness family–owned store in Bellevue, Ohio, making, at that point, close to $400 a year, a sizeable increase from his starting wage of $5 per month!

In 1853, at the age of twenty-three, Henry married Mary Harkness, with whom he had fallen in love while working for the Harkness family. They had three children, but both of their daughters died—Carrie at the age of three in 1861 (she was the younger daughter), and Jenny Louise at age thirty-four in 1889 following the death of her newborn daughter. In his great sorrow,

There were two railroads that initially served the Jacksonville beaches. While the Jacksonville, Mayport & Pablo (locally known as the "Jump, Men and Push!") is shown on the map, the more southerly narrow-gauge Jacksonville & Atlantic is not, although it would be purchased by Mr. Flagler and become part of the route used for the FEC's beaches branch. Shown here leaving the Jackson & Sharp Car Company Works in Wilmington, Delaware, in 1885 is Jacksonville & Atlantic combination passenger-baggage car #1, the Pablo Beach.

This is the only known Jacksonville, St. Augustine & Halifax River Railroad pre-Flagler purchase of the railroad-issued stock certificate that exists. (Unissued specimens are in collections, but there are no other issued certificates known). This, dated December 30, 1882, was for three hundred shares and was signed by railroad president A.M. Lyon.

Henry would build what is known today as the Flagler Memorial Church in St. Augustine, and both he and Jenny Louise are entombed there. In 1870, Mary and Henry's son, Harry Harkness Flagler, was born, and although he was close to his father, the elder Flagler's marriage to Mary Lily Kenan on August 24, 1901, created a schism between father and son that would never fully heal.

There is, of course, so much more to the early Flagler story, but, as noted, this is not intended to be another biography. However, the meeting of Flagler and one John Davison Rockefeller, occasioned by their working together in the grain and salt businesses, must be noted, for they, along with Samuel Andrews, would, in 1867, form the partnership firm of Rockefeller, Andrews and Flagler. Rockefeller, in his *Random Reminiscences*, would later write that his "relationship with Henry Flagler was a business founded on friendship, not a friendship founded on business." In 1869, the decision was made to incorporate, and with that decision, the name of the firm was changed to Standard Oil Company.

In February 1910, Edwin LeFevre interviewed Mr. Rockefeller for *Everybody's Magazine*, and one of the most revealing questions in the interview came when LeFevre asked Rockefeller if Standard Oil was his idea. In his usual straightforward manner, Rockefeller replied, "No sir, I wish I had the brains to think of it. It [Standard Oil] came about because of Henry M. Flagler." Many times throughout his life, Rockefeller would state, honestly and candidly, that "the key to our success was Henry Flagler." He also noted, according to William H. Allen's *Rockefeller: Giant, Dwarf, Symbol,* that it was Flagler's imagination and ingenuity that were responsible for the continued growth of the business.

Contrary to what has appeared on computer websites, Mr. Flagler's first visit to Florida was during the winter of 1878, not later. The trip to Jacksonville, which formerly had been known as Cow Ford, was an attempt to alleviate the ill health of his wife. While she improved in the warm Florida climate, the return to Cleveland and her discomfort and suffering throughout the following winter did nothing to help. In very early 1881, with Mary frailer then ever, Henry returned to Florida, this time to Orange Park. Although experiencing a slight improvement, Mary's body, without proper care or antibiotics, could not fight the ravages of "consumption" (which, at the time, was how any illness of the chest or lungs was known), and she died, much to Henry's sorrow, on May 18, 1881.

Once Mr. Flagler purchased the Jacksonville, St. Augustine & Halifax River Railroad, upgrading began almost immediately. By November 1892, the railroad had reached New Smyrna Beach, and plans were in place for extensions farther south, hence the name of the railroad was changed to Jacksonville, St. Augustine & Indian River Railway, reflecting the geographic reach of the line. Shown here is Jacksonville, St. Augustine & Indian River Railway parlor car Ponce de Leon, purchased from Jackson & Sharp in 1892.

Until the great freezes of the mid-1890s, which were the catalyst for the extension of the railroad south to Miami, the citrus belt began in Orange Park (named for that reason), just south of Jacksonville, and oranges and other citrus fruits were plentiful throughout north Florida. Dr. Garnett's orange grove in St. Augustine, shown here, was just one example of a part of the agricultural industry that now begins at Vero Beach.

Mary's nurse, for much of the duration of her illness, was Ida Alice Shourds. Shourds had been a kind and loving companion for Mary, and at the time of Mary's death, Ida Alice was only thirty-five. Her caring and attention to Mary had greatly impressed the bereaved Henry. Following an appropriate period of mourning, he began to see Alice socially, and he found her captivating to the point that he asked for her hand in marriage. With Ida Alice's assent, the couple was married on June 5, 1883, in New York City, and in December they left for a belated honeymoon in Florida. Staying for a short time in Jacksonville, they boarded a St. Johns River steamer, which took them to Tocoi Landing, where they disembarked and took the St. Johns Railway from that point into St. Augustine. It was that trip that irrevocably altered the future of Florida.

Fortunately for Florida—and for America—it was Flagler's imagination and ingenuity that caused him to make the decision to move to St. Augustine with Ida Alice following the 1883 visit, and it was that decision that changed the future and fate of the Sunshine State forever.

The remainder of the early years of the story—the building and buying of hotels in St. Augustine; the purchase of Flagler's first railroad (the rickety little narrow-gauge Jacksonville, St. Augustine and Halifax River Railway, purchased originally for the purpose of upgrading it so that goods and materiel destined for the then under construction hotels could and would reach St. Augustine in a timely manner); the extension to Ormond and the purchase of the Ormond Hotel; the building and buying of more railroads; the extensions to Daytona, West Palm Beach, Palm Beach and Miami; the building and buying of additional hotels; the founding of now great and world-renowned cities; the divorce from Ida Alice and the marriage to Mary Lily—are and have been the subjects of numerous books, booklets and articles. Hence, and again, it is not necessary to further detail those well-known facts.

Flagler's greatest single challenge, however, the one feat that would set his name apart from and above all others in Florida history and would enshrine the name of the Florida East Coast Railway in the great halls of American history, still lay several years in the future. When the time came, though, the only person in America capable of facing the task, fully cognizant of the obstacles and hardships that would have to be overcome in order to bring the Eighth Wonder of the World into existence, was none other than Henry Morrison Flagler.

2

"We Must Have a Railroad"

K ey West achieved its early fame and fortune due to several fortuitous
happenstances, and just as the previous chapter was not a biography
of Mr. Flagler but rather an overview of his pre-1903 life, this chapter, in
regard to Key West, will serve a similar purpose. This is not a history of
Key West, but in order to understand how and why the Florida East Coast
Railway was extended to the island city one must recognize the unusual
circumstances that brought about that herculean feat.

In 1822, following the confirmation of the treaty by which Spain formally
turned over Florida to the United States in 1821, Lieutenant Matthew C. Perry
(later gaining fame as Commodore Perry) planted the U.S. flag on Key West,
claiming the island and the entire chain of keys for the United States. Whether
or not that symbolic gesture was needed or necessary is a matter of conjecture.

Two years later, at the request of Lieutenant Perry, Commodore David
Porter, with approval by Congress, established and commanded a squadron
of fast sailing ships charged with ridding the West Indies of pirates.
Following this, he established a naval depot at Key West and made it his base
of operations, thereby instituting the first permanent U.S. military facility in
the Keys. In 1831, the army built a post on the island, which became home
to two companies of infantry.

First incorporated in 1828 as a city and then reincorporated as a town,
the island would see its first newspaper published in 1829: the *Register*, the

"There waren't much to it." Cocoanut palms along the shore line at Boca Chica Key, circa 1900.

first newspaper south of St. Augustine. Several newspapers would come and go, but by 1831, the closure of the *Inquirer* left the town without a newspaper until 1845, the year of Florida's acceptance into the union. During that year, the army began the construction of Fort Taylor, but hurricanes destroyed the completed post. Rebuilding began almost immediately, and in 1861, the not-yet-completed fort was occupied by the army.

One of the town's earliest occupations was that of wrecking and salvaging—the saving of passengers, crew and goods from ships that had wrecked on the reefs close to the various islands. Also important to Key West in terms of revenue-producing industries were sponging, turtling, salt production and, later on, cigar manufacturing.

With the outbreak of the Civil War, the United States moved quickly to secure Key West so that it would not fall into Confederate hands, and while a series of military commanders maintained order in the Keys, the major event of the war (as far as Key West was concerned) was the appointment of Judge William Marvin as federal provost marshal of the Keys. Judge Marvin, who was virulently antislavery, would brook no interference with his demands on the population of the Keys in general and Key West in particular.

The military barracks at Key West, circa 1904.

In 1863, shortly after assuming his post, Judge Marvin ordered all signs of Confederate sympathy destroyed, and the army moved from house to house to take down any flags or bunting that appeared to favor the South. At each business or dwelling that was found to have the offending paraphernalia, the military commanders ordered each of the males to sign an oath of loyalty to the union; failure to do so would result in confiscation of the property as a result of what, to Judge Marvin and the military, was clearly treason. There were no refusals.

But Marvin went a step further and ensured his place in Florida history by issuing a pre-Emancipation Proclamation edict: even though slavery in Key West was completely different from anywhere else in the South (there were, obviously, no plantations); even though many of the slaves did not live in their masters' homes; even though some of the slaves worked for other people (although tithing some of the remuneration to their masters); and even though several slaves actually owned their own businesses, Judge Marvin issued a non-appealable order dictating the end of slavery on the island. The military was ordered to carry out the edict in the most forceful manner necessary. On that day, Key West became the first Southern venue to end slavery.

Following the war, the constant unrest and turmoil (translated to "revolution") in Cuba caused many of the cigar manufacturers to build large factories for the production of their product and move their equipment and employees to Key West. By 1880, Key West, with almost ten thousand residents, was the largest city in Florida, a distinction the city would hold for almost forty years.

But what about the railroad? How and when did it enter the picture?

The first railroad in the United States, or at least the first to offer steam-powered passenger train service, was the Baltimore & Ohio, for which ground was broken in 1828. Two years later, in 1830, the first passenger service began. Incredibly, in 1831, only a year after the first railroad ran in America, and with Florida almost a totally and completely undeveloped wilderness (other than the small settlements in St. Augustine, Cow Ford,

Island City National Bank in Key West, circa 1904. The sender of this early postcard had some less than flattering comments about the city. Above the picture of the bank he wrote, "The city don't amount to much. To [*sic*] many people going and coming." Of course, at that time, it was the largest city in Florida, and the city fathers apparently believed that the city not only amounted to a great deal but also had a brilliant future if Mr. Flagler could be convinced to extend the railroad there.

Tallahassee, Pensacola and Key West), the first article propounding a railroad to the island city appeared in a newspaper. Obviously, that article was not taken seriously.

But what *was* taken seriously was the charter of the Great Southern Railway, incorporated in 1870 by the famed Confederate general John B. Gordon, for whom (after his death and of which he likely would not have approved) the Ku Klux Klan klavern (chapter) in Miami was named.

In 1878, with one R.P. Minear shown as president of the company, a hardbound 268-page book complete with a fold-out map of the proposed system tipped into the back cover and titled *Great Southern Railway* was published in New York by William P. Hickok, a stationer and printer at 93 Nassau Street. Without going into great detail, two items must be exhibited. In the frontispiece are the following words (we have not delineated lineage): "Great Southern Railway, A Trunk Line, Between the North and the Tropics, to within Ninety Miles of Havana, Connecting at the Nearest Possible Point with the West Indies, Central and South America."

But if that were not enough, the following words are on pages v and vi of the preface: "This railroad is designed to connect the entire railway system of the United States with Cuba, the other West Indies…and South America by the most direct and close railway and steamship connections that can possibly be opened. It begins at Millen (in Georgia)…and runs thence due south to Key West."

Numerous chapters, particularly the third, which is titled "Location of the Road," clearly state that the southernmost destination in Florida was to be Key West.

Likely due primarily to the Panic of 1873 and for various other reasons, only a few miles of the Great Southern were ever built, none of those anywhere near the central or southern portions of the state, and at that point the Great Southern simply disappeared from the annals of Florida history.

According to Professor Gregg Turner in his *A Short History of the Florida Railroads*, very little railroad building was done until the late 1880s concurrent with the appearance of "the three Henrys," the three great men—all named Henry—who essentially built Florida, but none of them had, at that time, any interest in or intention of building a railroad to Key West.

It would not be until June 1896 that the thought, concept and idea of a railroad to Key West would be taken seriously, for in that month the then

"We Must Have a Railroad"

Along with wrecking (salvaging), turtling and cigar manufacturing, one of Key West's most important industries in the late 1800s and early 1900s was sponging.

newly established *National Geographic* magazine published an article by Key West's famed and beloved collector of customs, Jefferson B. Browne, that was titled "Across the Gulf by Rail to Key West." Browne not only noted that the first survey of a rail route to Monroe County's seat was made by J.C. Bailey for the International Ocean Telegraph Company in 1866 but also essentially laid out a route that, interestingly enough, would be very similar to what William J. Krome would survey some eight years later and recommend to Mr. Flagler as the ideal right of way.

Browne's article concludes, "A railroad to Key West will assuredly be built [but] who will be its Cyrus W. Field? The hopes of the people of Key West are centered in Henry M. Flagler…The building of a railroad to Key West would be a fitting consummation of Mr. Flagler's remarkable career and his name would be handed down to posterity linked to one of the greatest achievements of modern times." Indeed, it would be, but only after the people of Key West and the Florida Keys were made to wait eight years for the announcement—for the building of the Key West Extension, which might instead have been the Cape Sable Extension, almost didn't happen.

Sometime in 1902, following the American government's decision to complete the Panama Canal and after conducting extensive studies that

An early view of Key West features the Custom House (at right, with flag flying, now the Custom House Museum of the Key West Art and Historical Society) and an abundance of flora, particularly coconut trees.

seemed to indicate that many, if not most, of the ships going through the newly opened canal in an easterly direction would head for the nearest deepwater American port for restocking and refueling, and believing that it was imperative that he tap what looked to be a lucrative new revenue stream, Mr. Flagler, with the input of his railroad vice-president, Joseph R. Parrott, and his land commissioner, James E. Ingraham (for whom the Ingraham Building in downtown Miami is named), made the decision to extend the railroad and build that port. While it may come as a horrific shock to many, that extension was originally destined for Cape Sable, at the very bottom of the state's west or southwest side, not for Key West.

Because that statement, like the debunking of the "orange blossom myth," flies in the face of conventional wisdom, this book will present documentation that will positively support the truth regarding the extension. Had the extension gone to Cape Sable and not to Key West, Mr. Flagler's legacy, while still remaining stellar and lofty, would not have achieved the sobriquet of "legendary."

Beginning at some point in the 1940s and continuing through the early 1950s, a man by the name of John S. Abercrombie was corresponding with, among others who worked on the extension and were still alive, Carlton

"We Must Have a Railroad"

Corliss. Abercrombie, living in Miami, began to collect material on and about the extension and, in fact, began writing a book about the great feat that he planned to title *Reporter in Paradise*. Mr. Abercrombie died without completing his work, and his files ended up in a Miami bookstore on Northeast Second Avenue called Bill and Dee's, from whence this writer, as a much younger man, purchased them. The Abercrombie material is of immense value, as his investigations and subsequent findings, complete with supporting material, prove, unequivocally, that Mr. Flagler's initial intent was to extend the FEC to Cape Sable and not to Key West.

In chapter eleven of his typewritten manuscript, Mr. Abercrombie notes that "it was never the intention to end the road at Homestead," going on to elaborate on the surveys of a route to Cape Sable, there being two of them, one conducted in 1902 and '03 and the other in 1904. Fortunately for posterity, the Bramson Archive is the repository of the FEC Railway blueprint of William Krome's survey across the Everglades to Cape Sable upon which, sworn to for its accuracy and validity by FEC chief engineer E. Ben Carter and certified by notary public George J. Zehnbauer, is the complete route of the seventy-eight-mile expedition conducted by Mr. Krome.

To further support the contention that the original destination was not Key West, the reader is referred to the February 9, 1904 edition of the *Miami Daily Metropolis* in which appears an article titled "Off to the Glades" with the following words leading off the article: "Mr. W.J. Krome, railroad engineer, with a party of twenty-three men, started this morning for the south to make a prospecting survey of the country below the present located line of the Cape Sable Extension of the Florida East Coast Railway." The article then goes on to note that "the railroad people want information as to the character of the country...in order to base their conclusions as to future developments."

The "future developments" were twofold. Upon returning from the 1904 survey, Mr. Krome, who had been somewhat reticent about stating his true feelings regarding that route to Mr. Flagler, decided that it would be dishonest and unfair not to be completely open with his employer, and when he was called in to meet with Flagler and other FEC officials regarding the completion of a route to the above-noted "nearest deepwater port," Krome said simply, "Mr. Flagler, there is not enough fill on the face of the earth to build a railroad across the Everglades."

Looking up Duval Street, circa 1903. Horses and buggies line the streets in front of First National Bank, right foreground. Behind the bank is the Jefferson Hotel, which, until 1901, was the FEC Hotel Company's Hotel Key West.

It was on that day, according to Carlton J. Corliss, who would become one of the construction engineers and an assistant to Mr. Krome and who would later go on to become the head of the public relations section of the Association of American Railroads and write several papers on the construction process, that Mr. Flagler turned to Mr. Parrott and quietly said, "Please arrange to have a survey made for a route to Key West."

On that day in early 1904, the fate and future of Henry Flagler, the FEC Railway, the Florida Keys and Key West would be forever and inalienably altered, and the beginnings of what would become the greatest railroad story ever told were nothing more than a survey away.

3

"Gentlemen: The Railroad Will Go to Sea"

It is easy to assume that, with management's approval of the survey of a route to Key West, the extension below the mainland and the choice of Key West as the terminal of the extension was a "done deal." It was not, however, and it would not be until the survey had been completed. When Mr. Krome returned from the task of surveying a route to Key West, he was ushered into Mr. Flagler's office at the Royal Poinciana Hotel in Palm Beach. "Mr. Krome," Mr. Flagler intoned, "what do you have to tell me?"

"Well, sir," Mr. Krome began, "we have completed the survey," at which point Mr. Flagler interceded.

"One moment, please, Mr. Krome. I gather that the survey has been completed, and I would be most appreciative if you would simply advise me of your findings."

Mr. Krome well knew that the boss expected a simple statement of facts, and he answered Flagler in kind. "Sir," he said, "it will be difficult, but it can be done."

It is possible that one version of the story of Mr. Flagler's approving the building of the extension to Key West occurred following Krome's short statement, noted above, when, according to Carlton Corliss, Mr. Flagler simply said, "Well, go ahead then." The problem is that there is no support for that version, as Mr. Flagler had not, at that point, gone to see for himself, and as we know from the numerous letters and documents relating to Mr.

This page: In taking the various trips that he made for the purpose of inspecting his railroad, hotel and other properties, Mr. Flagler would have traveled in his private or office car behind locomotives such as 4-4-0 #22 (shown with the engineer and fireman in front of it) or 4-6-0 #30 (shown here in its original Schenectady Locomotive Works engineer's side portrait).

Flagler's ownership and control of his various enterprises (the "Flagler System"), that was not the method or style of the "hands-on" manager Flagler was.

To use the "old saw," though, it was effectively a done deal, at least as far as the preliminary approval went. But before anything concrete in terms of the initiation of construction could occur, Mr. Flagler felt that it would be

"Gentlemen: The Railroad Will Go to Sea"

Chased deep into the Everglades during the three Seminole Indian wars, the remaining Native Americans survived by hunting, fishing and farming, only reluctantly rejoining civilization when Mary and William Brickell made it known that they would be welcome at the Brickell trading post on the south side of the Miami River.

Prior to the arrival of the first FEC train on April 15, 1896, Miami was a wilderness; one of the few solid buildings was the former U.S. Army Fort Dallas, shown here. The building was sold to Julia Tuttle, who converted it to her home and from there began the promotion of what would, some years in the future, become one of the world's great cities.

Flagler owned not only railroads and hotels but also land companies, newspapers and electric light companies, as well as other businesses. In 1899, the FEC paid $13.31 for "betterments" to the Miami Electric Light Plant, a Flagler company. The document is signed by FEC master mechanic George A. Miller and superintendent R.T. Goff.

Next two pages: In January 1900, the FEC published its annual *East Coast of Florida* booklet, describing, in words and photographs, the wonders and beauties of the on-line towns that it served. With the sun shining out of the clouds on the east coast of Florida, the tag line "The East Coast of Florida is Paradise Regained" became the company's mantra. The back cover of the booklet, which clearly shows the railroad's route, features the FEC Steamship Company's lines from Miami to Havana direct and to the Cuban capitol via Key West, hence an FEC presence was part of the Key West land and seascape beginning in the late 1890s.

necessary for him to tour the proposed route below Jewfish Creek—and that he did on the P&O Steamship Company's *Martinique*, which he and his party most likely boarded in Miami.

The Bramson Archive contains the record of that trip: according to the Peninsular & Occidental Steamship Company's invoice number 3070, dated May 26, 1904, and sent to the Florida East Coast Railway in St. Augustine from the office of the P&O's cashier in Jacksonville, the SS *Martinique* was chartered by "President H.M. Flagler and party, May 1st to May 3rd, 1904."

EAST COAST
OF
FLORIDA

The East Coast of Florida is Paradise Regained.

CITY GATES, ST. AUGUSTINE.

J. D. RAHNER,
ASSISTANT GENERAL PASSENGER AGENT,

J. R. PARROTT,
VICE-PRESIDENT AND GENERAL MANAGER,

J. P. BECKWITH,
TRAFFIC MANAGER,

ST. AUGUSTINE, FLA.

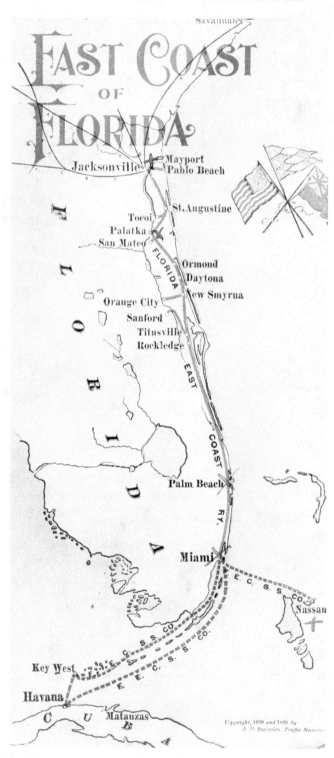

"Gentlemen: The Railroad Will Go to Sea"

The charge for the journey was $524.94 inclusive of crew pay of $124.30; provisions totaling $136.39; range coal, $6.00 (that for the coal stoves); steam coal (for the boilers), $249.75; and "Mineral Water etc." at a cost of $9.50.

On June 8, in a letter to the FEC's general auditor, W.H. Chambers, referenced "Trip of Martinique," Mr. Parrott approved the payment on behalf of the railroad. As always, there are skeptics who may wish to doubt that the trip on the *Martinique* was for the purpose stated above; however, the contents of the letter from Parrott to Chambers will forever put those doubts to rest, for in the letter Mr. Parrott wrote, "Dear Sir: Please note the attached bill from P&O SS Co. for $524.94 for use of 'Martinique' for trip to Key West May 1st to 3rd; you may voucher this *and charge to the Miami-Key West Extension.* [This is the first item known have been charged to the extension. Italics have been added.] Yours truly, J.R. Parrott, Vice President." The FEC's payment, with a voucher signed by Chambers and Parrott, was received by P&O's cashier, H.E. Osborne, on June 28.

Since the Flagler System was, at that time, 50 percent owner of the P&O (later purchasing the other 50 percent from the Atlantic Coast Line Railroad, which had gotten the half that belonged to Henry B. Plant [see Turner and Bramson, *The Plant System of Railroads, Steamships and Hotels*] when it purchased the bulk of the transportation assets of the former Plant System from Plant's wife, Margaret, and his son, Morton, in 1902), it was similar to taking money out of one pocket and putting it in the other, but even then, proper accounting procedures had to be followed. Apparently, Flagler liked what he saw on that voyage.

There is a great and apocryphal story that is as much a part of the lore and legend of the extension as any other tale, true or tall, and this story, which, it seems, occurred following Mr. Flagler's boat trip to assess and evaluate the planned route, has him standing on the very southernmost point of dry land on the Florida peninsula. In that location he is facing, according to the story, a semicircle of his top executives, including the aforementioned Messrs. Parrott, Ingraham and Krome, as well as the man brought in to be the chief engineer for the extension's construction, Joseph C. Meredith, who had built the massive docks at Tampico for the Mexican government, and the talented and highly regarded marine engineer Howard Trumbo, who would oversee the construction of the great terminal at Key West today known as "Trumbo Island." There was some brief small talk regarding the construction project, and then, at the clearing of his throat, the five men

By the 1904 season, the Florida East Coast descriptive booklets had already become larger and more elaborate, with full-color covers and the "paradise regained" phrase a prominent part of the advertising.

turned to face Mr. Flagler, who, even at that time, was accorded a near-godlike reverence.

Flagler looked at each of them and then partially turned, facing in a southwesterly direction. Raising his right arm, he pointed in an almost biblical manner and (according to the story) said, "Gentlemen: The railroad will go to sea."

As noted, this is an apocryphal story. It is not known whether there were actually six men present, and it is not known if the men, six or fewer, stood where it is said they stood. And, truth be told, it is not even known for certain whether Mr. Flagler uttered those immortal words, but one thing *is* certain: in the greatest railroad engineering and construction feat in U.S. (and possibly world) history, the Florida East Coast Railway went to sea, digging its way south of Homestead through the eighteen-mile-stretch to Monroe County and bridging Jewfish Creek (more like a fairly good-sized river than a creek), moving on to Key Largo and then jumping from island to island, building causeways and bridges and crossing bodies of water as long as seven miles wide, then, finally, eight long years later, reaching Florida's then-largest city on the most gloriously happy day in conjunction with the largest event in the city's history. Indeed, the Florida East Coast Railway was destined to become "the railroad that went to sea."

4

A Task Like No Other

It is fortunate for Florida historians, particularly those who are railroad and Florida Keys history buffs—and, more specifically, those who are FEC Railway aficionados—that there are, when it comes to the history of the building of the Key West Extension, two somewhat diverse types of researchers: those who are more interested in the memorabilia (photographs, timetables, booklets, brochures, badges, medals, souvenir china and other such pieces and postcards) than the statistics (how many tons of steel and how many pounds of concrete were used; how many board feet of lumber; how many nails; how many yards of rail; how much fill was used at Trumbo Island; how many buildings and where, exactly, they were; how many men were working at different times; how many boats were being used; etc.) and those who are more interested in those very arcane and sometimes difficult to compute with accuracy numbers that provide the basis for understanding the immensity of the task and the hugeness of the undertaking.

Frankly, as the senior collector of FEC Railway and Florida transportation memorabilia in America (June 2011 began my fifty-fifth year of maniacal, hysterical, fanatical and always filled with joie de vivre collecting), and as the company historian of the FEC, I am not hesitant to state that not only do we need both types of historians but also that we are blessed to have them.

As was noted in the introduction, this is not a book about the construction of the 128 miles of railroad from Homestead to Key West (mileposts 394 to

Miami, Florida, 7/14/04 1904

m M. J. Krome for F. E. C. Ry.

Bought of **Whaler's Jewelry Store**

Diamonds, Watches, Clocks, Jewelry

Musical Instruments and Strings

Rogers & Bro.'s Spoons, Forks, Etc.

No. 314 12th Street

Alarm Clock Pd 1.00

CHECK. T. WHALER, MIAM. FL. Paid

QUANTITY CORRECT

VOUCHER NO. 10628

J. M. Burdine   E. V. Quarterman

Pictures

Artistic Souvenirs

Leather Goods   Miami, Florida, 5/13   1904   Artists' Materials

Ladies' Furnishings   m M J Krome East Coast RR,   Perfumery

Ribbons   Novelties

Embroideries   Bought of **Burdine & Quarterman**   Sporting Goods

Stamped Linens   **Dry Goods**   Stationery, and

Embroidery Silks   Office Supplies

No. 308 Twelfth Street   Next Door West of Sewell Bros.

Terms Net Cash. Monthly Settlements

May 13 2 yd Oil Cloth 45 2 spools Needles 105

CHECK.

QUANTITY CORRECT

ORDER NO.

VOUCHER NO. 10628

Paid

This page: The proof of the fact that Mr. Krome was asked by Mr. Flagler to survey the route to Key West is told not by a written directive (there was none) but by the fact that, on April 24, 1904, Mr. Krome purchased from Whaler's Jewelry Store, at Number 314 Twelfth Street (now Flagler Street) in Miami, an alarm clock for $1.00, as well as, a month later, oil cloth, spools and needles from dry goods merchants Burdine & Quarterman for $1.05. Simply put, Krome had no other reason to be in Miami at that time other than to begin to make preparations for the great task that lay ahead.

522) but rather the story of the incredible twenty-three years and just less than eight months' existence of that part of the railroad from beginning to end. As the reader may have noted, the first three chapters lead up to this chapter, which discusses that great feat, but this chapter is not meant

as the be-all and end-all for facts and information on the construction. Rather, the point and purpose of this chapter is to provide the reader with an understanding and an overview of—in the context of the entire Key West Extension story—what the builders of the extension faced, how they overcame the trials and tribulations that made the construction so incredibly difficult and how, eventually, they would, on January 21 and 22, 1912, bask in the glory of the arrival of the first two trains to make the through trip from the mainland to the island city.

There are three major works on the construction portion of the story that must be noted. The first is the book titled *Florida's Great Ocean Railway: Building the Key West Extension* by Dr. Dan Gallagher, considered the premier reference on the construction and engineering portion of the extension. The second reference is the senior thesis done by Todd Tinkham in 1968 at Kalamazoo College in Michigan in partial fulfillment of his bachelor of arts degree requirement titled "The Construction of the Key West Extension of the Florida East Coast Railway: 1905–1915." The third is *Speedway to Sunshine: The Story of the Florida East Coast Railway*, which is the official history of the railroad.

Both books and the thesis were heavily drawn upon (along with the material and memorabilia in the Bramson Archive) for facts and information during the preparation of this chapter, and I have attempted, wherever feasible, to specifically note from which source information is presented, as well as to delineate the source of other references as they are used.

Although both Gallagher and Tinkham seem to agree that construction— the actual physical labor relating to the building of the railroad—began in 1905, neither they nor others who have written about the extension have noted that, according to the company's official announcement of the opening of the extension, published in conjunction with the arrival of Mr. Flagler's train on January 22, 1912, "Joseph Carroll Meredith was appointed Chief Constructing Engineer and entered on his duty the 22nd of July, 1904…His plans were laid months in advance of the work and practically every detail for the final completion of the work had been put on paper."

The implication and logical assumption, therefore, is simply that, while the actual physical labor may have begun, again according to the official announcement, "south of Homestead in 1905 under the immediate charge of Mr. Meredith until his death, the 20th of April, 1909," the beginning of

This page: J.C. Meredith (top) was the chief engineer for the massive project until his untimely death during construction, at which time William J. Krome (bottom) became chief engineer. It was he who would see the extension through to completion. *Both images courtesy of the Monroe County Public Library*.

the great project can be dated to the day in July 1904 that Meredith accepted responsibility for completing the enormous task.

Sometime in 1908, he wrote in his diary the following prophetic words: "No man who can not stand grief should be connected with this enterprise." Less then a year later, Joseph Meredith was dead, the victim of the grief connected with that immense and, to some extent, brutal enterprise.

Obviously, construction could not have started without the assemblage of men and materiel, boats, ships, various pieces of railway equipment and, of course, the necessary right of way and property to allow the construction not just to begin but also to continue unabated throughout the project. That work began in 1904 following Meredith's employment, and because of that, the statement that the construction of the Key West Extension began in 1904 is completely correct.

The die had been cast, and the stage was set. Henry Flagler had figuratively thrown the dice, and with that roll unknowingly prepared himself to become a legend—a larger-than-life character—in his own lifetime. The fortunes of the Florida Keys—of Key West—had, prior to that roll, hung in the balance. But with the roll of those dice, Henry M. Flagler became Florida's Empire Builder.

Although initially various parties appeared to be responsible for different purchasing tasks, the fragmentation of that job, along with the difficulties arising from not having a central supply and equipment planner and purchasing person, brought Mr. Flagler to the realization that the delays and subsequent inefficiencies the engineering and commissary staffs were incurring were simply unacceptable, and he vowed to make the necessary changes.

In 1906, Flagler reached out to a longtime acquaintance from Cleveland, one Frank Rogers (this is the first time in any book, article or publication on or about the extension that that name has appeared, mostly because Rogers's daughter, the late Margaret Grutzbach, maintained the confidentiality of her father's position and role with the railroad until our fortuitous meeting in 1986) and convinced him to join the railroad as the chief steward for the construction of the extension. Rogers was highly trained for this role, as his responsibilities would include overseeing all purchasing and distribution of all material used on and by the railroad, from coal, ties, track and spikes to floating equipment, steel, concrete, wood and food service items. Rogers is the unsung hero of the building of the extension, and to no small extent the memorializing of his name is long, long overdue.

As noted above, the story of the engineering for and construction of the extension has been told in numerous articles and several books, but Dr. Gallagher has repeatedly emphasized the importance of two locations as the actual construction headquarters: the P&O docks in Miami, which were the jumping-off point for the project and the place where, according to Gallagher, "Meredith and the project team [which would have included Frank Rogers] had their administrative offices...and they ran the project from Miami until March 1909, when the control center moved south to Marathon."

As the extension moved south, Gallagher has taken pains to note the great role that Marathon played as the major construction complex, which included Knight's Key Dock, Boot Key Harbor machine shop and the town of Marathon itself, complete with hotel and recreation facilities for visiting reporters and other dignitaries. That complex also included the central engineering offices and distribution depot. Besides utilizing several marine railways at Marathon to service the various boats and ships that made up the construction fleet until 1916, Knight's Key Dock served as an international port of entry from 1908 until 1912, when the line was opened from Knight's Key to Key West.

While the construction was moving inexorably south and southwest, the railroad, on three different occasions, faced the worst of the horrors of the tropics: terrible hurricanes. The first was on October 17, 1906, the second on October 9, 1909, and the third in October 1910. Numerous sources, including Abercrombie, Gallagher and Tinkham, address the storms—Abercrombie noting all three, Gallagher giving specific details on the 1906 and 1909 events and Tinkham detailing the 1910 hurricane. (The 1935 hurricane, which destroyed the extension, is covered in *Speedway to Sunshine*, the late Pat Parks's *The Railroad that Died at Sea* and at least two other books, as well as a good few articles, and will be detailed in this book in chapter twelve.)

Dr. Gallagher, in *Florida's Great Ocean Railway*, notes that most of the deaths of railway employees during the 1906 storm came when Quarterboat Number Four, home to between 131 and 160 men, was ripped from its moorings during the storm and carried toward open water, apparently breaking up when it crashed into several completed piers near its Long Key dockage as it was swept out to sea. Another casualty was the paddle-wheel steamboat *St. Lucie*, which went down with the loss of at least another twenty men. Although not noted in some of the articles on the construction, it appears

A 243-foot span is being put in place on Bahia Honda Bridge during construction.

that, in total, there were at least 200 men killed as a result of that terrible storm, and the railroad learned well from it how to prepare for the future.

After the 1906 hurricane, canals were excavated at a number of sites to provide safe anchorage from the storms, and the crews were no longer kept on the houseboats (quarterboats) but were, instead, moved into safer shelter in permanent structures on the islands.

The 1909 storm resulted in fewer than twenty deaths, thirteen of them occurring when the tugboat *Sybil* capsized at Bahia Honda and, according to Tinkham, a few men were killed when they were apparently caught near the embankments, although no exact location is given.

The 1910 hurricane was described by conchs as the worst, up to that time, in Keys history. Corliss, in his *Building the Overseas Railway to Key West* (published in 1953 in volume thirteen of the Historical Society of Southern Florida's *Tequesta*, its yearly journal), notes that the engineers and foremen, having received proper and early notice of the onrushing terror, were able to secure boats and all railway equipment in the maelstrom's path so that damage to railroad property was kept to a minimum and only one life was lost.

After each hurricane, first Meredith and then Krome would wire Flagler with a list of the losses and an appraisal of the situation. Each telegram ended with the question, "What would you like for us to do?" And in each case, without hesitation, Mr. Flagler responded, "You will continue the work and complete the railroad to Key West."

For FEC fans and buffs and oversea railway historians, it just doesn't get much better than this. An aerial view of West Summerland Key shows the entire layout of FEC construction-era buildings on that key. It is quite likely that the small building at the end of the pier to the right of the pilings is the outhouse or, in today's terminology, the "comfort station."

By 1908, construction had reached Knight's Key, and at that point, for the next four years, all trains would terminate at a dock (Knight's Key Terminal) located about one-quarter of a mile east of the right of way, literally out in the Atlantic Ocean. Opened officially on January 15, 1908, the terminal, upon which construction had begun in January 1906, had two tracks running the approximately six-hundred-foot length of the dock. The length of the trestle work, from the point it left the west end of Knight's Key abutment and then swung under Span 36 of the Knight's Key Bridge, was about thirty-eight hundred feet. Hence, the trains moved over almost three-quarters of a mile of open water to reach the temporary terminal.

The "permanent" track, replacing the temporary trestle out to Knight's Key dock, opened on January 22, 1908. In early April, the dock was connected to the mainland by telephone, and a U.S. post office was opened later that month. The dock, which was seventy-five feet wide, functioned almost independently, with a small hotel, a train shed, quarters for employees working on the dock, a dock master's office and some locomotive servicing facilities.

Oceangoing freighters would tie up at the dock, and passenger boats of the P&O Steamship Company connected Key West with the trains terminating at Knight's Key for the four-year existence of the terminal. Railway post office service was established, with the clerks leaving the train southbound at Knight's Key and continuing on to Key West on the P&O boat; they would reverse the procedure northbound. This was an arrangement that ended on

Sometimes, once in a great, great while, something relevant to the oversea railway surfaces that is so outstanding and so incredible that it must be remarked upon and held in reverence. This incredible photo of the Marathon Bath House and Dock was made by none other than H.H. "Hy" Hyman, and best of all, there is a message on the back from Hy to his family telling them that what is on the photo is "our club house and our auxiliary that the company lets us use."

January 22, 1912, with the beginning of through trains carrying railway post offices running to and from the mainland.

The number of boats and ships used in the construction of the extension seems to be eternally in question, but fortunately, the Abercrombie manuscript provides a fairly good detailing of the Flagler fleet:

> *A practically complete list of the boats used on the job shows that there were twenty-seven launches of from five to fifty horsepower; eight stern-wheeled steamboats brought down across the Gulf from the Mississippi River; three tugboats; twelve dredges; eight cement mixers for work on the water...nine pile drivers for water construction...one catamaran for handling cofferdams; eight derrick barges with capacity from ten to thirty tons; one hundred and fifty lighters for sand, gravel and cement; two steel barges, 136 feet long and one of thirty-six foot beam, each of which could handle forty car loads of material at one time; and two seagoing steamers for conveying cement in bulk.*

In the Bramson Archive, there is yet another listing, this one handwritten by an unknown individual who attended a talk by Mr. Corliss on April 8,

1953, in which he noted that Corliss stated that there were sixty launches and fifteen houseboats.

Unquestionably, though, Dr. Gallagher, in his *Florida's Great Ocean Railway*, has done an incredible service to any fan of the FEC, particularly of the extension, as chapter three in that book is titled "Vessels of the F.E.C." and the discussion of the boats used covers every kind and type, complete with photographs of many of them. As far as the launches go, the actual number appears to have been more than sixty. Gallagher goes so far as to show the names of sixty-three launches with this notation: "The following list of launches includes only the ones for which known documentation and published specifications exist," thereby implying that there may have been more and other boats in that category.

It should also be mentioned that, besides the more obvious impediments to working smoothly and moving ahead as rapidly as possible with the project, including ferocious mosquitoes, hurricanes, a high turnover of men and, in the summer, heat and humidity, along with making certain that the men had good, wholesome food and all the water they needed, the railroad was faced, in 1907, with charges by two disgruntled employees of "white slavery" and a claim that the railroad was holding workers in bondage and not allowing them to leave.

In 1908, *Leslie's Weekly* did a major article, written by Hamilton Houston, addressing the contretemps. The article debunked the charges, complete with seven photographs under the heading "Photos that Disprove a Lurid Tale of White Slavery in Florida," the photographs showing, among other scenes, Mr. Flagler, Mr. Parrott and other executives inspecting the work; the laborers' mess hall on Windley Key; the emergency medical tent at Camp 4; and a large number of men gathered for payday at Plantation Key. It noted, too, that not only had the government wasted $300,000 on prosecuting claims that were dismissed by the federal judge hearing the case but also that the railroad had to spend $300,000 to show that the charges were completely baseless and without merit or validity.

With all of this written, it is now necessary to note that time was moving rapidly. Mr. Flagler was aging—he would turn eighty-one in January 1911—and was beginning to falter.

Near the end of February 1911, Krome received a letter from Parrott. "The Chief is failing," Parrott wrote, "and it is imperative that you speed up the construction." Parks, in *The Railroad that Died at Sea*, states that Parrott

This page: During construction there were, apparently, several thousand views made of the work and the facilities. Among those are the highly desirable and very rare "F.E.C. Railway Extension Series" postcards, a numbered set unendingly sought by collectors of the genre. Shown here are two of the cards, including #21, which is "Suction Dredge Rough Rider at Work, Upper Matacombe [*sic*], Fla.," and #29, "Fresh Water Supply Barge Taking Water, Manette [*sic*; this was Manatee] Creek, Fla."

asked if Krome could finish the road by January 2, 1912, "so that we can put Mr. Flagler there [into Key West] in his private car over his own rails on his next birthday." Krome wrote back that he could do it by January 22, "should no storm overtake us or no unforeseen delay set us back."

In order to achieve that goal, nearly a year was cut from the construction schedule, and the work timetable moved to a twenty-four-hour-per-day basis, the railroad generating its own electricity for the after-sundown labor and men working ceaselessly to see to it that Henry Flagler would live to see the great goal achieved and to ride in his own railroad car over his own rails behind a locomotive lettered for his own Florida East Coast Railway.

Parrott said to Krome, "Make it so," and indeed, Krome saw to it that the job was done.

Once again, it is to be noted that the details of the construction of the oversea railway are worthy of the several books that have been written on the topic, and those who have dedicated themselves to that task are deserving of the honors they have received for recording in detail the incredible event and for the accumulation of facts and material that was something only extremely determined individuals could have pursued. But before we close this chapter by paying tribute to—and thanking—the men and women who provided the information and have written the books and articles on and about the incredible feat of building the Key West Extension, we must also inform our readers that the extension was *not* anywhere near complete on the greatest day in Key West's history.

In fact, and as shown in the various books on the topic, as well as in the numerous accounting sheets and forms charging expenses to the proper department(s) that now reside in the Bramson Archive and are dated from 1912 through 1916, the Key West Extension, as a separate accounting entity of the FEC Railway, continued to accumulate charges until all the temporary trestles were either filled or rebuilt with permanence, all of the structures were acceptable for long-term usage and all of the trackage and right of way had been completely tamped down and inspected for the use of freight and passenger trains, a service that began on Monday, January 22, 1912. It would not be until 1916, however, that the construction work on the extension would be completed and the separate accounting books that were maintained for the extension as its own entity would be closed.

Now, though, with time marching on, it is necessary for this book to move forward to the greatest single day in the history of Key West. And that day, of course—a day in the making for seven and a half years—would occur on January 22, 1912.

5

"I Can Not See the Children but I Can Hear Them Singing!"

Without stealing any thunder from Key West's day of days, it is important to note that as early as 1907, two steam locomotives were actually assigned to the Key West terminal, and they were kept busy almost from day one moving carloads of rock, fill, sand, gravel, riprap, marl, steel, construction supplies and concrete into the proper place for unloading to be used either on the causeway across Garrison Bight, which the railroad would use to reach Trumbo Island, or for filling in the area that would physically connect the terminal to the city.

During the pre-1912 construction phase, the city grew by 134 acres as Howard Trumbo directed the placement of fill for the terminal site, as well as for use for storage of the construction supplies and material brought in by the steamboats. Gallagher relates, "Initially cement was stored in Key West [but] later the shipments went directly to the Knight's Key dock."

The building of the extension was not, as some have supposed, a linear task, with mile after mile following in order; rather, it was the result of superb planning and the ability of Frank Rogers to respond quickly to the requests that came in on a daily basis for the purchase and distribution of vital supplies and equipment.

The engineering and construction team was headed by Joseph C. Meredith and, following his death, by William J. Krome. It was these two leaders who would bring together the superb group of men who, for the

It is possible that the number of images of the crowds and of the arrival of the passenger trains into Key West (particularly the first train, carrying Mr. and Mrs. Flagler and their party) on January 22, 1912, could very well reach several hundred. However, at the time of the publication of this book, there is only one photo known to exist that actually shows the engine number of the locomotive bringing Flagler's train on to Trumbo Point, and that is the photo shown here, with #48, a 4-4-2 type, built by Schenectady Locomotive Works in 1901, leading the train toward the Key West depot. A navy honor guard is visible to the right with the crowd behind it. A member of the engine crew, possibly the road foreman of engines, is leaning out of the gangway on the engineer's side of the engine, waving to the well-wishers standing on the left side of the train.

most part, remained loyal and faithful to the project and, because of their dedication, were able to see the work through to completion.

Memorialized in numerous publications, P.L. Wilson, C.S. Coe, Krome, Ernest Cotton, general foreman Edward Sheeran and bridge engineer R.W. Carter are pictured together on the rear of an observation car in what may be Marathon in *Speedway to Sunshine*. Their names, along with those of Henry "Hy" Hyman (belying the anti-Semitic nonsense that has been bandied about regarding Mr. Flagler, the FEC had employees of the Jewish faith beginning as early as 1898, and Mr. Hyman was one of the highly valued members of the engineering corps; as one of the assistant chief engineers under Mr. Krome, he later became the first Jewish employee of Florida Power and Light Company, eventually rising to the rank of vice-president), W.A. Glass, James Dunaway and William A. Venable, are forever enshrined

"I Can Not See the Children but I Can Hear Them Singing!"

A somewhat distant view of Mr. Flagler's train on its arrival in Key West gives the reader an idea of the enormity of the anxiously waiting crowds.

in the annals of Florida's railroad history for what they did to help bring Mr. Flagler to Key West.

Although several passenger trains would arrive in Key West on Monday, January 22, 1912—with Mr. Flagler and his invited party on the first of those trains to come to a halt at the newly constructed depot at exactly 10:43 a.m. behind steam locomotive number 48 and with Florida governor Albert W. Gilchrist on the last of the day's trains to burnish the rails on that glorious day—the fact is that the very first train to make the complete trip from Palm Beach through Miami and on to the island terminal did so the day before, on January 21.

It was on that day that Mr. Krome and his fellow engineers, leaving Miami very early in the morning with a group of roustabouts and gandy dancers (track workers), proceeded to Homestead, where they may have stopped for a brief breakfast. From Homestead, at a speed of no more than ten miles per hours, they rolled slowly down the Keys, inspecting every inch of the rail and roadbed and stopping to spike each switch into the open (main line) position, for on the following day the chief would make his grand and triumphant entry into Key West, and that trip had to be perfect.

According to Martin, the first train to make the complete trip was piloted by William Nichols (he may have been the road foreman of engines), while locomotive engineers J.F. Norton and Ed Goehring, with Jack Basskopp serving as fireman, had the honor of bringing that train from Miami to Key West.

Mr. Krome had coordinated the schedule of construction to the point that, shortly after his train left Miami, the last two steel deck plates needed to actually complete the line were brought out to Knight's Key Bridge span 36 on barges, and after disassembling the wooden trestle leading to Knight's Key dock, the cross bracing was put in place, the ballast was tamped down and the cross ties were laid with the track spiked to them, all in the manner of a well-oiled machine and completed well before Krome's train was scheduled to arrive at that point.

Once the first part of the trestle was removed, the dock was left in place until after Mr. Flagler reached Key West, which he would do on the following day. Several weeks later, after all usable material had been removed, the Knight's Key dock became part of Florida Keys history as it was sprayed with kerosene and then burned to the water line.

Although some revenue began to flow into the railroad's coffers once the Knight's Key terminal opened beginning in early 1908, the fact was that the outlays were immense and far greater than the revenues. Yet every penny was accounted for, as is shown, for example, on the "Extra Labor Pay Roll" forms, which were kept for every day of operation. A full box of them currently resides in the Bramson Archive. (These forms were used in all stations and by all FEC departments, as necessary).

An example of the Knight's Key payroll for non-salaried employees ("extra labor") for the period from October 1 to October 10, 1909, indicates that twenty-one employees worked 1,644 hours, all at the then quite generous rate of fifteen cents per hour, and the railroad paid out $246.60 in wages in the first ten days of October 1909 for those in the "extra labor" category at Knight's Key alone.

It is interesting to note that each employee signed for his pay on the extra labor payroll sheet. If he was illiterate, he would make an "X," and the person witnessing the signature would write "His Mark" above or below the "X." Other months showed similar expenditures, and for the month of June 1909, for example, the railway paid $552.40 to its extra labor employees in the course of the entire month. The payroll sheets were sent to general auditor Chambers in St. Augustine after being approved by Knight's Key's agent R.H. Whitnall or his successors and then signed by either vice-president J.P. Beckwith or Mr. Parrott.

"I Can Not See the Children but I Can Hear Them Singing!"

While it is common knowledge that Mr. Flagler and his party were greeted by Key West mayor Dr. J.N. Fogarty; chamber of commerce president George W. Allen, who presented Flagler with a silver and gold tablet bearing his likeness as a gift from the citizens of the city; and the Key West Navy Yard's Admiral Lucien Young, it is not common knowledge that the first hand that Flagler shook upon being helped off his train upon its arrival on that joyful Monday was that of his chief steward, Frank Rogers. And the story, as told by his daughter, Margaret Grutzbach, fits with all that we know about his arrival.

Rogers moved to Miami from Cleveland in 1906, when Margaret was six. Margaret and I met when she called the Jerry Wichner radio program on WINZ, which was an AM station at 940 on the dial. I was Jerry's single most frequent guest, and the phones lit up all night when I was on (Jerry was Miami's "midnight mayor," and we were usually on from 11:00 p.m. till 5:00 a.m.), as all the older folks and the insomniacs would call in to talk history, whether it was Miami trolleys, the FEC Railway or South Florida in general. We would also discuss other U.S. railroad and streetcar history.

One night in early 1986, a woman with a sweet, soft voice and a wonderful Florida cracker accent called in. The engineer said, "Jerry, Margaret on line four." Jerry greeted her, and she said to Jerry, "Hello, Jerruh, may I speak to Mr. Bramson?" I pushed my phone button and said, "Hello, Margaret, this is Seth," to which she replied, "Mr. Bramson, my name is Margaret Grutzbach, and we moved to Myamuh in nine-teen-oh-six when I was six years old." I asked her why her family had moved here in 1906 and where they had come from, and that was when she "dropped the bombshell."

"Mr. Bramson," she repeated, "we moved here in 1906 because Mr. Flagler hired my daddy to be the chief steward for the construction of the Key West Extension." At that point, my knees became weak, primarily because in the introduction to the original *Speedway to Sunshine*, which was published in 1984, I had written the following words: "The story of the FEC is, unlike that of most railroads, a 'modern' story, taking place primarily within the twentieth century. Even today, there are people alive who remember, with clarity, Mr. Flagler's arrival in Key West."

When I finished the introduction, I called Myrna, who was in the kitchen baking, to come into the den and hear what I had written. When I read that second sentence to her, she stopped me and said, "Are you sure? Are you sure

Closer to the train and the depot, a corner of which is visible on the left side of this image, this view again shows the assemblage with the navy's honor guard standing between the crowd and the seven-car train. One of the Key West switch engines is on a track to the left, waiting for the festivities to move to other locations so it can begin shifting the cars and turning the trains for their return to the mainland.

that now, seventy-two years later, there are people alive today who were there when Mr. Flagler arrived in Key West and who still remember? Are you sure?" And I answered her hopefully, saying, "Well, I sure as hell hope so!" We both smiled, and that ended the conversation until the night of Margaret's call.

After Margaret told me who her father was, my first question was, "Did he take any pictures of the construction?" And her incredible answer? "Oh, yes, Mr. Bramson, and I still have his albums!" At that point, Jerry had to help me up off the floor! I asked Margaret if she had ever gone to Key West, and her answer put me back on the floor.

"Mr. Bramson," she said, in that sweet, soft voice, "you know that it was verruh dangerous work, even for my father, and he only got up to see us about once every other month, but on January 18, 1912, he came up to Myamuh by boat, and when he got home he said to me, 'Margaret, honey, how would you like to come to Key West with me on the twentieth, and then we can go to the station and see Mr. Flagler come in on the fust train on the twenty-second.' 'Oh, Daddy,' I replied, 'that would be wonderful!'" Of course, having written what I had in the *Speedway to Sunshine* introduction, my response was, "Thank God," because there really was somebody alive who remembered with clarity Mr. Flagler's arrival in Key West!

"I Can Not See the Children but I Can Hear Them Singing!"

This page: There were two major publications issued for the opening of service on the extension. The first was published by the railroad and is the *Announcement*, a thirty-two-page, heavy-stock-cover, cord-bound, five-and-five-eighths- by eight-and-three-eighths-inch booklet with a map of the terminal as the frontispiece and an eastern U.S. map featuring Florida and the FEC on the rear of that page. The booklet concludes with a foldout featuring the Flagler Hotels on the front page and on the back of that promotional, three photos of the construction complemented by a two-panel map. The second publication was the beautiful book issued by the Over-the-Sea Railroad Celebration Committee, which was sold to those interested for the grand sum of twenty-five cents a copy. Seven by nine and seven-eighths inches with eighty pages and a foldout map of the FEC tipped into the inside back cover, this beautiful volume is one of the most sought-after pieces of FEC Railway memorabilia that exists.

"We got up bright and early on the twentieth, which was a Saturday, and took the boat to Key West. I don't remember much about the trip, but we got into Key West, and we stayed in a very nice place that Daddy said was owned by the railroad. On Saturday, Daddy took me around and showed me the city and it was just fascinating." By now, of course, my pupils were dilating.

Margaret continued:

> We got up bright and early on Monday morning and we had a nice breakfast and went to the station where a huge crowd had already assembled. You know, Mr. Bramson, Daddy was a very important person with the railroad, and we went right up to the station. Fairly early we could hear the fust whistle of Mr. Flagler's train, and the crowd went wild, cheering and singing and crying with joy. Each time we heard the whistle it was louder and the crowd [estimated at over ten thousand people] got louder as the train got closer. Finally it came into sight and then, slowing down, came right up to the station.

"Did you get to see Mr. Flagler?" I asked.

"Why, Mr. Bramson, when Mr. Flagler was helped off the train, the very fust hand that he shook was my daddy's, and then he put his hand on my head and said, 'Margaret, have you been a good little girl?'"

At that point, we ended the call, with me shaking like a leaf in a rainstorm and my whole body soaked with perspiration. Fortunately, Jerry's engineer made certain that he had Margaret's phone number. Two days later, as I sat with her and talked about her experiences with a father who was of major importance to the success of the Key West Extension construction, Margaret gave me Mr. Rogers's albums, from which I made negatives of every image. When I returned them to her, she told me how happy she was about my interest in history and very kindly presented to me, as a gift, the letter Mr. Parrott had written to Mr. Rogers in February 1913 in response to Mr. Rogers's expression of sympathy following Mr. Flagler's death.

While from time to time we read stories or hear of people whose great- or great-great-grandfathers or grandmothers had shaken hands with Abraham Lincoln, President Grant or General Lee, I imagine that, at the present time, I am one of the few people on earth who was hugged by, and in return

"I Can Not See the Children but I Can Hear Them Singing!"

hugged, a person who had been touched by Henry M. Flagler. Other than marrying Myrna and having two spectacularly great grandsons and a fabulous niece, I really don't think that it gets any better than that.

There are no few stories of Flagler's arrival, of his being escorted by the mayor, Mr. Allen and Admiral Young to the reviewing stand while Key West's children, all wearing white, walked backward in front of him, singing and strewing roses in his path. Whether true or not, the story that he turned to the mayor and the chamber president and said, "I can not see the children but I can hear them singing" is a story of legendary proportions, as is what he supposedly said to Mr. Parrott once he was escorted onto the reviewing platform: "Now I can die fulfilled." Whether or not he said this is immaterial, for, accompanied by his third wife, Mary Lily, he was the center of attention and the main attraction for the entire remaining portion of the Over-the-Sea Railroad Celebration, sponsored and hosted by the committee of the same name made up of various military and civilian Key West bigwigs.

The parties, honors and accolades were endless, and the names of the balls and various tributes have been well recorded; hence, it is not necessary to repeat those names. But what *is* necessary to note is that, following the completion of the extension, the employees of the railway presented Mr. Flagler with a magnificent gift (what do you get for the man who has everything?) of a thermometer, barometer and chronometer in a beautiful housing, which is now safely and lovingly ensconced in Palm Beach at Whitehall, the Henry M. Flagler Museum.

Mr. Flagler was deeply touched by the gesture, and on January 27, 1912, he wrote the following letter (the original of which is now in the Bramson Archive) from his office in the Royal Poinciana Hotel in Palm Beach to Mr. Parrott, who by then had become president of the railroad while Mr. Flagler had risen to the position of chairman of the board:

> *Dear Mr. Parrott: The last few days have been full of happiness to me, made so by the expressions of appreciation of the people for the work I have done in Florida. A large part of this happiness is due to the gift of the employees of the Florida East Coast Railway. Their loyalty and devotion is evidenced by the beautiful gift they have sent me and for which I beg you will express to them my most sincere thanks. I greatly regret that I cannot do it to each one in person.*

With no "railroad buff" types on the scene at the time, nobody thought to take individual views of the passenger cars or the locomotives. Hence, the only known photograph in which the lead steam engine's number is visible is above. Regretfully, while there are close-ups of the cars, the numbers or names are simply not visible. In this view, Mr. Flagler is holding his hat just to the left of the lower center of the photograph. It is believed that the man immediately behind him is either Joseph R. Parrott or chamber of commerce president George W. Allen.

The work I have been doing for many years has been largely motivated by a desire to help my fellow-men, and I hope you will let every employee of the Company know that I thank him for the gift, the spirit that prompted it, and for the sentiment therein expressed.
Very truly yours, [signed in ink] *H.M. Flagler.*

The *Official Program and Souvenir: Key West Extension of the Florida East Coast Railway*, which was published, as noted, by the Over-the-Sea Railroad Extension Celebration Committee and is filled with stories, advertisements and information, also contains the "Program of Key West Celebration" listing each of the events that were to be held, including, besides all of the balls and receptions, parties, parades and fireworks, "Aviation by the Glenn H. Curtis Aviation Company, Famous Aviators" (Curtis would have a major impact on Greater Miami in the great boom years of the 1920s, co-founding Hialeah and founding the cities of Miami Springs and Opa Locka) and a "Grand Contest Dance and Reception by the Y.M.H.A. (Young Men's Hebrew Association)."

"I Can Not See the Children but I Can Hear Them Singing!"

A close-up view of the greeting party shows Mr. Flagler shaking hands with Admiral Lucien Young shortly after his arrival. Frank Rogers, chief steward for the construction, was the first person to shake Flagler's hand as he stepped off the first train, and Flagler graciously spoke to Rogers's daughter, Margaret, putting his hand on her head and asking her if she had been a good little girl. To Admiral Young's left is Key West mayor Dr. J.N. Fogarty, and it is believed that the person holding Mr. Flagler's left arm is either Mr. Parrott or chamber of commerce president George W. Allen. Mrs. Flagler (Mary Lily) is to Henry's right holding the large bouquet of flowers, but her face is blocked by the admiral's cap.

Another individual who had the good fortune to be present when Mr. Flagler arrived was Celeste Archer, later Celeste Sanchez, of Key West. Celeste, her brother and her father and mother, Mr. and Mrs. George Archer (he a Key West banker and a member of the Over-the-Sea Railroad Extension Celebration Committee), are in several of the photographs showing Mr. Flagler being escorted from the train to the reviewing stand.

Having purchased the FEC Railway and Florida railroad memorabilia collection of one Frank Fontis, who claimed to own the property at 512 Greene Street in Key West on which he was planning (for many years) to open the Old Coffee Mill and Florida Railroad Museum, from Mrs. Sanchez—who actually *did* own the property—following Fontis's untimely death on New Year's Day 1980, a letter written by Mrs. Sanchez to her friend Margie (no last name is shown; the letter was addressed "Dear Margie" and dated February 6, 1973) was included with the memorabilia.

In the letter, Mrs. Sanchez points out, in a photograph in her possession, Mrs. Flagler (who, according to Key West Art and Historical Society executive director Claudia Pennington, was shown wearing only black dresses while in Key West because of the recent death of her mother) and names Sam Roberts, Mrs. Archer holding Dorothy Archer, Celeste's sister, Edith M. Leuthi (in the letter Mrs. Sanchez notes that Mrs. Leuthi is shown in the picture with a white spot on her nose, likely from the photographic process) and her father. In front of them, holding on to Dorothy's baby carriage, is Ruth Knowles. Mrs. Sanchez then goes on to note, "Standing behind Mr. Flagler's rear and Dr. Fogarty's tummy is Celeste herself."

Celeste then goes on to relate that she chose that vantage point as she was ready to dart out and pick up the bouquets that the Flagler procession had passed. The rest of the letter talks about health issues that she was facing, including the reconstruction of her hand. Fortunately, when I met her in the early 1980s and made the arrangements to purchase the Fontis collection, she was in excellent health, her memories of the railroad in Key West clear, crisp and completely intact.

Following the celebration, and upon returning to his Palm Beach home, Flagler continued to work, looking after events affecting his empire and graciously accepting laudatory public comments, as well as receiving regular payments in amounts ranging from $50,000 to $250,000 on account of the hotel company, the land companies or the railway. He was able to look back on an incredible life with pride and pleasure, though certainly he could not have known, at the time of his death, that he would become the most revered person in the history of the Sunshine State.

Early in his eighty-third year, descending not the great marble staircase at Whitehall, the magnificent home he had built in Palm Beach for Mary Lily, but rather the private staircase located underneath the grand staircase (which he preferred to use when Mary Lily had her gala parties), he slipped and fell, breaking his frail hip. Unlike today, when hips are easily replaced, there was no known treatment, and all the doctors could do was sedate him and try to keep him comfortable. They notified his son Harry, who was in New York, but by the time Harry reached his father's bedside, it was too late. The elder Flagler was unable to communicate.

On May 20, 1913, Henry Flagler died. Two days later, every employee, every train and every piece of machinery and equipment on the Florida East Coast Railway stood still and at attention for ten minutes to honor the memory of Florida's Empire Builder. Henry Morrison Flagler was, simply put, one-of-a-kind, and, truth be told, there will never be another.

6

The Magnificence of
the Bridges

At various times over the years of the life of the extension, the FEC would include, in its passenger timetables, a condensed list of the extension's bridges. Additionally, in the privately printed (no attribution is given as to author or publisher and no date of publication is shown) booklet titled *The Overseas Railroad*, which at one time was sold in gift and souvenir shops along the overseas highway, several of the bridges are noted, and their approximate lengths are given. Gallagher and Tinkham also provide information on those incredible structures, and Frank Patterson, writing in the *Railway Age Gazette* of May 10, 1912 (republished by the FEC as *The Florida East Coast Railway/Key West Extension* in a four-and-a-half- by nine-inch horizontal-format booklet later in 1912) provides a great deal of information on several of the bridges and their construction.

Pat Parks shares some details, as does Abercrombie. It appears that, along with the list shown by the railway itself in its passenger timetable number three for July 12, 1928, the reader will find that he will be able to avail himself of those sources as an as-close-to-complete list as possible, not only of the bridges, but also of their lengths and locations. It should be noted that the FEC timetable referred to above shows only the longer spans and bridge structures, the shortest on that list being 399 feet in length, so the reader should be aware that the shorter bridges are likely shown or at least referred to in several other books, booklets or brochures that, although not

While not the only one of the Keys bridges constructed with arches, the Long Key Viaduct seems to have been the most graceful, as well as the most photogenic, and it was selected by the railroad for use as its emblem on all timetables and stationery for the years of the extension's existence. In this marvelous photograph by FEC company photographer Harry M. Wolfe, a thirteen-car Havana Special, being pulled by one of the FEC's fast passenger service 400-series, 4-8-2-type steam locomotives is en route to Key West, complete with the Pullman lounge/observation car on the rear of the train with seven people standing on the open platform.

company issued, are just as valid for use as information sources as the FEC Railway's timetables.

The FEC timetable bridge list comes from page fourteen of the above referenced schedule, and on that page, which features a picture taken on the deck of the Seven Mile Bridge with no land in sight, the headline below the photograph says, "The Over-Sea Extension," and below that is the following text:

> *A trip across the Florida East Coast Railway Over-Sea Extension is one*
> *of the most unusual railway journeys in the world. At times one has all the*
> *impressions of an ocean journey by train. In crossing the longer viaducts*

The Magnificence of the Bridges

Although not often remarked upon, Rockland Viaduct, at milepost 513.2 (nine miles north of Key West), was 1,231 feet long and was another of the arch-construction-type viaducts.

land is almost lost to view and the distant keys appear as faint ribbons of green on the horizon. The matchless tints and colors of the clear subtropical water defy description.

The Over-Sea Extension, which is more than one hundred miles in length, links the mainland of Florida with Key West. The famous Havana Special, traversing this route, makes direct connections at the Island City with steamships to and from the Cuban Capital.

In addition to a large number of long fills, the Over-Sea Extension includes the following principal bridges and viaducts [what follows is the list of the bridges and viaducts of 390 feet or more, with both the mile post number and the length of the bridge, as shown in the July 12, 1928 timetable referred to above]:

NAME OF BRIDGE	MILE POST	FEET IN LENGTH
Channel No. 2	450.1	1,721
Channel No. 5	451.3	4,520
Long Key Viaduct	457.4	14,190
Toms Harbor Viaduct No. 3	461.3	1,210

NAME OF BRIDGE	MILE POST	FEET IN LENGTH
Toms Harbor Viaduct No. 4	462.2	1,397
Knight's Key Bridge	467.1	35,711
Little Duck Missouri Viaduct	483.3	800
Missouri-Ohio Viaduct	483.7	1,395
Ohio Bahia Honda	484.4	1,005
Bahia Honda	486.8	5,005
Spanish Harbor Viaduct	489.3	3,312
Pine Channel North Viaduct	493.5	622
Pine Channel South Viaduct	494.2	808
Torch Key Viaduct No. 1	495.0	799
Torch Ramrod Viaduct	495.4	616
Niles Channel Viaduct	496.7	4,435
Kemp Channel Viaduct	499.3	993
Bow Channel Viaduct	502.6	1,303
Park Key Viaduct	504.3	779
North Harris Viaduct	505.2	390
South Harris Viaduct	506.5	390
Lower Sugar Loaf Viaduct	507.5	1,212
Saddle Bunch Viaduct No. 2	508.4	552
Saddle Bunch Viaduct No. 3	508.7	656
Saddle Bunch Viaduct No. 4	509.8	801
Saddle Bunch Viaduct No. 5	510.3	805
Sharks Key Viaduct	511.3	1,989
Rockland Viaduct	513.2	1,231
Boca Chica Viaduct	516.4	2,573

While it is not within the purview of this book to list all of the bridges and their respective lengths, a discussion of the three mightiest and most imposing spans is something that should certainly be elaborated upon, and that discussion follows.

Before entering into that somewhat technical area, however, I recognize that the reader will likely want to know, at the least, how many bridges and fills there were between Homestead and Key West, as well as how many rotating spans or drawbridges there were.

The total number of bridges—from the first bridge, the 233-foot-long crossing of Jewfish Creek, which took the railroad from the mainland to

The Magnificence of the Bridges

Key Largo, to the last bridge, which was the drawbridge at Garrison Bight, leading the railroad from Key West over to Trumbo Island—totaled forty water crossings on the route.

The other four draw- or swing-span bridges, which were south of Jewfish Creek, included the briefly used Indian Key Draw at MP 445. It was a true drawbridge and was in place for and during the construction but was removed and replaced with solid fill prior to 1916, as it had a tendency to malfunction on a regular basis. The third bridge, which was a bascule drawbridge, was the Channel Five Draw, between MP 451 and 452. The fourth movable bridge was the majestic Moser Channel crossing, at MP 479, which, like the Jewfish Creek crossing, was a rotating swing-span bridge, not a drawbridge.

The last of the movable bridges, like Moser Channel complete with bridge tender's house, was the 159-foot-long Garrison Bight crossing at MP 521, one mile from the extension's last milepost, which was on the steamship dock adjacent to the Key West depot. The Garrison Bight Bridge took the railroad from the northernmost part of Key West over to the railroad's terminal on Trumbo Island.

As stated above, there were three bridges that would certainly, today, be entitled to the sobriquet of "breathtaking," whether for their beauty, their uniqueness in terms of structure or their length.

The first of the great bridges was the Long Key Viaduct. This beautiful and graceful bridge was, according to an article in *Dun's International Review* for April 1926, "a remarkable structure of the arch type, with 180 semi-circular concrete and steel arches and fifty foot span."

Perhaps the best description of the Long Key Viaduct appeared in the *Engineering Record* for November 23, 1907. Written by FEC engineer William Mayo Venable, the article detailed the construction of that structure, which was built in a channel from nine to seventeen feet deep. The arches had to be heavily reinforced with steel rods, and a unique method of construction for that bridge had to be adopted, with all work done from floating equipment.

All supplies for the Long Key Viaduct, according to Venable, were brought by water from Miami, including lumber, pilings and broken stone, all of which was unloaded at Knight's Key Dock and from there was brought to the various construction sites along the 14,190-foot bridge on barges towed by one of the sternwheelers. The gravel used on that job was brought in from Alabama and the cement from New Jersey and Germany.

In late 1926, in one of the era's most famous publicity stunts, Claude Nolen, of Nolen-Brown Motors in Jacksonville, arranged with the FEC to drive a new 1927 LaSalle the entire length of the Key West Extension. Shown here on one of the concrete bridges, Nolen is driving while the film crew, which recorded the complete trip, is in the vehicle following. FEC photographer Harry Wolfe took various shots during the trip; those negatives are now preserved in the Bramson Archive.

Once the sites for the piers had been chosen and marked, a floating derrick was used to lower a cofferdam at each pier location, and the process of pouring the cement began following other preparations, all of which were discussed in Venable's article. One thing that Venable made clear was that the complexity of the construction, which was a first in American bridge building, required thirty-three forms to be used in each of the 180 arches.

Venable, according to Corliss, kept impeccable and detailed records on each step of the construction in which he was involved, even going so far as to note in the *Engineering Record* that "the work force employed on the Long Key Viaduct varied from 500 to 800 men" and that "distance from the labor market and depots for machine supplies caused some delays."

Upon its completion, the viaduct was a tourist attraction, with people coming from distant points to see and photograph it. The FEC's management, struck with the uniqueness and beauty of the span, incorporated the image of a passenger train on the viaduct heading north toward Long Key and the Long Key Fishing Camp as its emblem. The design appeared for the first time as an actual photograph of a steam locomotive pulling a four-car passenger train on the cover of timetable number 98, dated January 7, 1913, less than one year after the extension opened. The June 1, 1913 timetable carried the same photograph, but the next several timetables, through number 105 for January 6, 1914, carried, as the cover photos (one on each side), sports images. Number 105 had views of golfers teeing off on the eighth tee on the Ormond Hotel course on the front cover, with "Tennis at Palm Beach" as the back cover photo.

By 1914, the decision had been made, very possibly by the company's passenger traffic manager, J.D. Rahner, that the passenger train on the Long Key Viaduct was to be the company's (or at least the passenger traffic department's) emblem, although shortly thereafter it began to appear on all FEC stationery and most company publications. (Rahner's name first appears on FEC timetables as a passenger traffic department official prior to the turn of the century, and he would remain with the railroad as its chief passenger traffic officer until shortly after the inauguration of the railway's first streamlined trains in December 1939.)

Rahner was not only a contemporary of Mr. Flagler, working directly for him as well as for Mr. Parrott, but he also served with the railroad from the days of wooden passenger cars and small 4-4-0-type steam locomotives through double tracking, the purchase of all new heavyweight equipment and massive 4-8-2 steam locomotives in the 1920s to and through the receivership and then the heady and hopeful days at the end of the Great Depression when the FEC and the Atlantic Coast Line Railroad purchased their first diesel locomotives for use on their new streamliners. One (a joint FEC-ACL operation) ran from Miami to New York, and another, an FEC train named Henry M. Flagler, operated as an intrastate express and made a daily Jacksonville-Miami round trip in thirteen hours.

Timetable number 109, dated November 15, 1914, carried the new symbol of the railroad. The stylized passenger train was shown at speed on the viaduct, with waves lapping at the bases of the bridge's arches in the center of an inner and outer circle. In a crescent around the top of the interior of the circle were the words "Florida East Coast Railway," and in a reverse crescent within the lower part of the double circle appeared the words "Flagler System." Below the circle, for some years, a scroll-like design that appears to be somewhat of a shield, carried as its legend, within a rectangular box, the words "The Over-Sea R.R.," and below that was a pair of palm fronds with a seashell between them. Several years later, the shield, the palm fronds and the seashell would be eliminated from the emblem, and a pair of two link chains would drop down from the circular emblem with the rectangular box attached to it, the words "The Over-Sea R. R." still within.

From that day forward, until the July 1, 1936 timetable was issued, not only would that symbol remain the FEC's emblem but also "The Over-Sea R.R." would become the way the railroad would be internationally known, with the Key West Extension often referred to as "the eighth wonder of the world."

Beginning in 1936, when it became evident that the extension—with the railroad in bankruptcy, traffic at a bare minimum, unregulated competition for the car ferries coming from the ports of New York and New Orleans and the United States in the throes of the worst financial crisis in its history—would not be rebuilt, the FEC's striking Long Key Viaduct emblem was changed to a beautiful sunrise over an ocean shore with palm trees in the background. "The Over-Sea R.R." box never appeared on FEC brochures, booklets or timetables again except in one 1945 operating department booklet that was somehow published with the no-longer-in-use symbol on its cover.

The company, cognizant of the value and importance of the oversea emblem decided, during the great Florida boom of the early to mid-1920s, that along with the new passenger equipment it was purchasing—which included a group of then-modern heavyweight dining cars for its great fleet of passenger trains—the hollowware that it was buying from the International Silver Company for those diners would have on the side of each piece or on top of the piece (if the item was a tip tray or a crumber) the oversea railroad emblem. That was the only hollowware used by the company until the flatware, with an earlier style of lettering, and the hollowware with the oversea railroad emblem on it were phased out as the railroad started purchasing streamlined passenger equipment beginning in December 1939.

A good bit of the oversea railroad–era hollowware was transferred to the FEC Hospital in St. Augustine, and some was taken home by employees. An unknown amount was melted down in the scrap drives for use in World War II, and an equally unknown amount is now in the hands of FEC Railway or dining car memorabilia collectors, the Bramson Archive being the repository of at least thirty pieces.

The second of the great bridges was the Bahia Honda Bridge, which was either 5,055 feet in length (FEC passenger timetable, July 12, 1928) or 5,056 feet in length (Sidney Walter Martin, *Florida's Flagler*) and connected Bahia Honda Key and Big Pine Key.

Bahia Honda means "deep bay" or "deep water" in Spanish, and indeed, the water in the channel at that point is the deepest encountered in the Keys. At low tide, the water is over twenty-four feet deep, and the concern of the engineering staff was that the water's depth at that crossing could seriously impede salvage or rescue operations in the event that an accident or derailment could result in a situation in which a locomotive or the cars of a train might either leave the track or fall from the bridge.

The decision was made to utilize truss spans for the length of the bridge, and that was the only bridge on the extension with protective sides. The same

The draw span on Seven Mile Bridge, shown in the open position. In another great Harry Wolfe photo, one can clearly see the ladder under the bridge tender's house that he used to access the building.

issue of *Dun's International Review* noted above reported, possibly erroneously, that Bahia Honda Bridge was built with thirteen through truss spans, each of those 128 feet in length, but Tinkham and Gallagher disagree.

Tinkham quotes from *A Railway across the Sea* by Stephen J. Hunter, in which Hunter (and, in turn, Tinkham) states that the first thirteen through truss spans were each 138.0 feet long. Gallagher, in *Florida's Great Ocean Railway*, notes the length of the same thirteen spans to be 128.5 feet long, an interesting discrepancy between eminent historians. At any rate, all seem to agree that the next thirteen spans were each 186.0 feet long, but the length of the center span appears to spawn another conflicting measurement. The center span referred to above was, according to both *Dun's* and Tinkham, 247.0 feet long, but again, Gallagher differs. He puts the length of the center span at 247.5 feet, but to paraphrase an old saying, "What's half a foot among friends?"

In addition to the truss spans, there were nine plate girders, each eighty feet long. Some of the support piers of the bridge were sixty to eighty feet long and solidly set in ocean bedrock.

The material used in the construction of Bahia Honda came from widely separated sources and regions. The trap rock was brought down from the Hudson River in New York State, while the cement, which hardened under water and resisted saltwater corrosion, was brought by freighter from Germany, as there was no American cement at that time that could harden in the underwater pressure.

There were, according to Gallagher, three hundred men working on Bahia Honda in early January 1912, when the bridge was completed in time for the first train on January 21. Engineer Venable's notes indicate that the work at Bahia Honda continued long after the extension was in operation, as much work needed to be done to shore up the approaches. Dredge operators worked continuously to pump in large amounts of additional marl to build up the approaches on both ends of the bridge. Gallagher indicates that "in 1914, a set of 18-inch thick concrete retaining walls were built on the west side of the bridge; these walls" he adds, "extended from the abutment down the length of the West Summerland Keys."

According to longtime FEC employees Harold K. North, who retired as assistant general passenger agent in Miami, and Arthur Marsh, who spent many years in the accounting department of the railroad in the St. Augustine headquarters and was the first person known to have collected

The Magnificence of the Bridges

and preserved FEC memorabilia, those fortunate enough to have had the opportunity to ride FEC passenger trains on the extension would audibly "ooohhh" and "ahhhh" when they went over the Bahia Honda Bridge as they did when they crossed both Long Key Viaduct and Seven Mile Bridge.

The third of the "big three" FEC bridges had to be saved for last, primarily because it has earned the greatest number of superlatives and is the giant of them all, stretching 35,711 feet from one end to the other. Known as Knight's Key Bridge or the Seven Mile Bridge, the structure is often referred to as simply "Big Seven."

The Seven Mile Bridge is often thought of as one bridge, but the fact is that it crosses Pigeon Key, that tiny speck of land about a mile south of Knight's Key, and when it was built, it was divided into four segments: Knight's Key Bridge, Pigeon Key Bridge, Moser Channel Bridge and Pacet Channel Viaduct. Dr. Gallagher writes that "the bridge we now call the Seven Mile Bridge was never called by that name while the construction project was under way; the name apparently evolved sometime in the 1930s."

Whether it is referred to as Knight's Key Bridge, Seven Mile Bridge or by any other name, the fact is that it is one of the most awe-inspiring feats of bridge building ever attempted and completed in world history, and while such entities as the Chesapeake Bay Bridge/Tunnel and the twenty-something-mile-long bridge connecting Sweden and Denmark are incredible in their own rights, the fact is that when Seven Mile Bridge was conceived and built, nothing like it had ever been attempted in the annals of American railroad bridge construction. While railroad bridges had already crossed the Mississippi, those simply went, no matter the length (and none anywhere near as long as seven miles), from one shore to another. The Knight's Key Bridge went, literally, out to sea.

Steam locomotive engineers and firemen, as well as passengers and both freight and passenger train employees, waxed rhapsodic at a trip over the Oversea Railway. Comments such as "I couldn't see land from the middle of the bridge" were common from those fortunate enough to have enjoyed a trip from Homestead to Key West. Passengers told of relishing a meal in one of the FEC's heavyweight dining cars while the train rolled over the bridges at a speed not exceeding twenty miles per hour, and they reported seeing schools of fish, porpoises jumping as the train passed, fishermen in small boats waving at them and glorious hues of ocean and gulf color.

Harry Wolfe, in one of the most breathtaking Key West Extension photographs ever made, climbed up to the bridge tender's house on Seven Mile Bridge and then, looking north, captured a vista that truly deserves the accolade "stunning." There are five men working on the track with their motorcar "parked" directly below the camera. The tiny island in the distance is Pigeon Key, and beyond that, almost completely out of sight, is the island at the north end of the bridge, Knight's Key.

There is, sadly, a rapidly dwindling number of those who still have memories of having made the trip over the extension, for as time inexorably rolls forward, even the magnificent bridges, out of railroad service since September 2, 1935, and out of highway usage since they were replaced (in some cases, several times) by automobile bridges within the last quarter of the twentieth century, are becoming victims of the waves, wind, water and weather. Unmaintained even as monuments to a great and incredible moment in time, they are deteriorating daily, fading slowly as they erode, untended and uncared for but hopefully never unremembered.

7

Right of Way and Stations

It is at this juncture that this book moves away from and beyond all of its predecessors, for beginning here, this book starts to cover much of what has never before been examined closely by historians or put into a book format until now. And that, of course, concerns what happened from the conclusion of the construction to and through the hurricane of 1935.

As has been previously noted, the Key West Extension remained a separate accounting and operating unit until 1916, with two steam locomotives assigned only to construction work on the extension. A number of the construction engineers continued their daily routine along the Keys for those four years and were assigned a group of maintenance employees who were working, for the ensuing four years following the arrival of the first trains into Key West, to actually complete the construction. As has been stated previously, in no few cases the viaducts and bridges were temporary and had been put into place so that Mr. Flagler's train (and Mr. Krome's the day before) would be able to make a complete and uninterrupted trip from the mainland to Key West.

While Mr. Flagler's death was not unexpected following his terrible fall at Whitehall, Mr. Parrott, as his successor, was expected to serve the railroad for a good few years to come. Sadly, he was to follow Mr. Flagler in death on October 14, 1913. The *New York Times*, in reporting Parrott's death the next day, stated that he had died suddenly of angina pectoris, a disease marked by brief paroxysmal attacks of chest pain precipitated by deficient oxygenation of the heart muscles, which apparently led to a heart attack. Parrott died at his home in Maine, where he had been vacationing, and apparently, none of his closest associates knew that he was suffering from a serious form of angina. It was the second terrible blow to the railroad in one year, with its two greatest leaders dying barely nine months apart.

William H. Beardsley, the treasurer of the Flagler System and a close, personal friend and confidant of both Flagler and Parrott, was the ideal and obvious candidate to replace Parrott. And this he did, remaining as president of the railroad until early 1924, when he retired. Beardsley, who had been with the Flagler System for many years, died at the age of seventy-three on December 13, 1925, and was succeeded as president by Flagler's brother-in-law, William R. Kenan, brother of the late Mary Lily. Kenan had, for some years, been a member of the Flagler System board and was vice-president of various units of the system.

Once the operation of the extension as a separate accounting unit was concluded in 1916, the line from Miami to Key West would become, for

When construction began, two dredges worked their way north from Jewfish Creek toward the end of track near Detroit (Florida City) by literally digging out the muck and floating themselves north. This marvelous view is an indication of what the future right of way looked like prior to the dredges beginning their work. *Courtesy Phyllis and Steve Strunk.*

operational purposes, the fifth division of the railroad. The extension's personnel included depot employees, bridge tenders, porters and baggage handlers, trainmasters, road foremen of engines, conductors, engineers, firemen, brakemen and trainmen, clerical personnel (at Homestead and at Key West) and, equally important, maintenance of way foremen and their section gangs. The foremen were assigned sections, and each was responsible for approximately twenty miles of track, which he and his crew were to maintain to the highest standards.

The original rail, which was laid for the opening, was replaced several years later with heavier ninety-pound rail (ninety pounds to the yard), and that was what was used for most of the years of the extension's operation.

Signals were not an issue, as the line below Miami was never equipped with electric light block signals and was operated strictly with train orders that were handwritten by agents at the several stations, named below, which were what was referred to as "agency stations." Although operating without color light signals, there were men assigned to maintain the telegraph lines that were the primary form of communication, along with the written train orders, along the right of way.

Key West was, of course, assigned the largest number of employees, and the station there was, until the coming of the Depression in 1929, a beehive of activity. While the other depots and their locations will be noted in this chapter, the Key West station, as part of the Trumbo Island Terminal, will be more fully discussed in chapter nine.

In addition to the railroad employees, there were also employees of private companies or government agencies who worked on or in proximity to the railroad. Among those were the express company agents and package handlers; the railway post office clerks, who worked the mails in either direction between Fort Pierce and Key West; the customs and immigration people at Key West; and the train "butchers" of the Union News Company and its predecessors, whose agents worked the trains selling newspapers, magazines, playing cards and other sundry items, including sandwiches and nonalcoholic beverages, the latter two items being sold mostly to coach passengers to consume at their seats as in some cases they preferred not to avail themselves of the dining cars. The Pullman Company also maintained an office at Key West where its sleeping car conductors and porters could check in and out before or after trips.

One of the smallest depots was at Jewfish, spelled on the sign as two words. The rudimentary condition of the right of way indicates that the building was opened shortly after the railroad reached that point. Ed Strum (this might be a misspelling; it might be Ed Strunk) and H.C. Penny are the men shown on the rail velocipede in the photo. *Courtesy Monroe County Public Library, Key West.*

Much of the ballast on the FEC's right of way, whether on the mainland or in the Keys, was Ojus rock, mined in and brought from Ojus in the northeastern section of Dade (now Miami-Dade) County. For some years, two companies, Ojus Rock and Maule Rock, supplied the ballast, and for a number of those years, as many as fifty carloads a day of that rock would leave the quarries headed for usage on the FEC, as well as other railroads or for other purposes. Although there are no buildings remaining of the quarry operations, the lakes and bays that are east of Biscayne Boulevard in what is today the city of Aventura are the remains of the rock company's years of dredging operations there.

Ties were then placed in preparation for the rail-laying operation, and in the days during and after Flagler's 1912 arrival, rail laying continued

Islamorada Depot was as substantial as those on the mainland. While the group in the photo is not identified, it is clear that, with restrooms reading "White" and "Colored" behind the men, segregation was in full force in the Keys at that time. *Courtesy Barbara Edgar and the Eyster family.*

unabated, as the Key West yard needed to be completed and shipper's sidings had to be put in place. Once the rail was spiked down (and all of that done by hand) and secured, the section foremen and their gangs were responsible for maintaining the trackage and the right of way in their respective sections.

The reader should now be made aware that there is a distinct difference, in railroad parlance, between a station and a depot. The former is any named location at which a train may stop, but that station may not necessarily be the site of a building or any actual physical facilities for passengers to use while they are waiting for their trains or after detraining. In fact, south of Florida City and north of Key Largo, there were two stations that were no more than lightly surfaced gravel areas without even the amenity of a wooden platform to be used as a waiting area. Those two stations (not depots) were Wooddall and Everglades (later known as "Glades"), and they are shown in the FEC timetables as "flag" stops, which meant, of course, that if the passenger wanted the train to stop, he had to wave a handkerchief (or his arm) in the daytime, or a bright light at night, to indicate to the engineer that he was waiting for that particular train.

Those two stations, incidentally, as well as the station called Jewfish at MP 415, were used almost exclusively by hunters and fishermen and, interestingly enough, saw a surprisingly regular stream of passengers boarding and detraining with fishing or hunting gear and a good bit of camping accessories rather than the regular luggage carried by most passengers.

The other type of station is a depot, and these are stations at which there is some form of physical accommodation for passengers, in some cases as minimal as a shed to protect them from rain, but in most instances with at least a sheltered waiting room.

Most of the FEC depots on the extension operated without an agent but did have shelter for passengers, and many may have had restrooms, which in the days of segregation would have been separated by race. All of the

Sitting on their handcar with the Key Largo right of way quite visible are FEC engineers Cox, Coe and Malone. *Courtesy Monroe County Public Library, Key West.*

stations are shown in the image of the FEC's timetable. In that timetable, an "f" indicates a flag stop, as discussed above.

In order to gain an understanding of how many station stops there were, it is best to, as the great line from *The Wizard of Oz* goes, "begin at the beginning." And though we shan't "follow the yellow brick road," we can and will follow the chronological progression of the timetables as they take us from the first actual extension service on January 22, 1912, to and through the last, before the September 2, 1935 storm ended service (that schedule folder being dated May 18, 1935).

On January 22, 1912, the FEC listed twenty-four stations between Detroit (later Florida City, the station immediately south of Homestead) and Key West, including Key West in that count. Quarry, Central Supply, Midway, Cooks Siding and Crescent were names that would not last long in terms of the ongoing issuance of the passenger timetables.

By June 1, 1913, there were twenty-nine stations listed between Detroit and Key West. Crevallo at MP 448 took Midway's place at that location; Toms Harbor was added at 460, three miles below Long Key; Bahia Honda was added at MP 486 between Marathon and Spanish Harbor; Ramrod Key was added at 496, between Big Pine and Cudjoe; Sugarloaf was added at MP 503 between Cudjoe and Chase; and Stock Island was added at 518, between Big Coppitt and Key West.

With the publication of timetable 105 on January 6, 1914, it appears that the station list had stabilized; there remained twenty-nine named stations between Detroit and Key West, with Key West included in the list but not Detroit, which was on the mainland and was the last depot facility before the station stop at Key Largo depot. Glades (which started as Everglades) and Wooddall, as has been noted, were mainland stations without any kind of facilities.

There are certainly no few readers who enjoy statistics and who, if space were not an issue, would enjoy seeing a list of stations for each timetable issued. While it would not be a problem to simply list every timetable issued by the FEC from January 1912 through May 1935 and enumerate each and every change in extension stations in terms of names and mile post locations, the ponderousness of that task, as well as the space it would take, even though the concept is excellent, would reach a level of such near-infinite detail and require such an inordinate amount of time that the completed book would likely not reach the publisher in time for the great centennial event on January 22, 2012.

Because of that fact, the more logical step is to simply select several different years and show any changes that may have occurred from one period to another, as was done above with the timetables from 1912, 1913 and 1914. Hence, the next timetable to be examined will be the December 2, 1925 issue, put out at the height of the great Florida "boom" for the 1925–26 winter season. Besides the two passenger trains that operated daily between Jacksonville and Miami, as well as the freight service over the line, the 1925–26 season would see a third Key West train added to the schedule and twelve trains daily operating between Jacksonville and Miami, including the two trains that went to Key West. The third train that was added to the Key West service originated in Palm Beach, crossed Lake Worth, backed into the West Palm Beach station on the wye that had legs on either side of the station and then headed south to Miami and the Keys.

The crossing at Caribee Colony on Islamorada. Owned by Eunice Peacock Merrick's parents, she and her husband, George Merrick, founder of Coral Gables, would take over the management of the camp following the 1920s bust in Greater Miami that bankrupted Mr. Merrick.

The December 2, 1925 timetable listed thirty-one stations, two more than are shown in the 1913 and 1914 timetables. The additional stations in that timetable are Thompson, at MP 427, between Rock Harbor and Tavernier, and Channel Five between Rossmore and Crevallo at MP 451. Several name changes are also evident: Central Supply is shown in that timetable as Matecumbe; Cook's Siding has been changed to Channel Five; Crescent, between Cook's Siding and Long Key in 1914 was changed to Rossmore; Tom's Harbor, which had been at MP 460 between Long Key and Grassy was no longer in the timetable; Pigeon Key at MP 478 appears as a conditional (flag) stop for trains 37 and 38; and Torch Key at MP 495 was added between Big Pine and Ramrod Key, a move that was extremely unusual, as Torch Key and Ramrod Key were only one mile apart. Boca Chica had been added at MP 515, but Stock Island, at MP 518, had been removed from the timetable.

Fortunately, the Bramson Archive does have some material related to station name changes on the extension, and when those name changes were made, or stations closed or opened or fares changed, the passenger traffic department would issue a bulletin regarding said changes.

An excellent example is Circular 35-8 (Supplementing Local Passenger Tariff 17), File MI-589, issued by general passenger agent J.D. Rahner on January 1, 1935, and from which the following information is gleaned: "'Channel Five' located at Mile Post 451.6...has been changed to 'CRAIG.' Fares quoted to and from 'Channel Five' now quoted in Local Passenger Tariff No. 17 and effective supplements will apply to and from 'CRAIG.'"

When a station name was changed, and if there was a structure of some kind, the paint gang would be notified and would, as expeditiously as possible (paint gangs were located in Miami and Key West), repaint the depot name signs at either end of the building. In some cases, if, for example, the name change was done to accommodate a local fishing camp or business and the sign was to be repainted at the request of that entity, the business requesting the name change would ordinarily bear the cost of either the repainting or the new signs, or both. Another example of a local business having the closest station bear its name is below.

Following the September 2, 1935 hurricane, the several timetables that were issued through 1936 carried the oversea railway emblem on their covers while noting that "service south of Florida City [was] indefinitely suspended." However, the last timetable issued by the FEC prior to the hurricane was dated May 18, 1935, and in that timetable there were only seventeen stations listed between Florida City (the former Detroit) and Key West, including the latter but not the former. Those stations and their milepost numbers are as follows:

Glades (Wooddall no longer shown)	408
Jewfish	415
Key Largo	417
Rockharbor (one word, as shown)	424
Tavernier	431
Plantation	434
Islamorada (Caribee Colony)	440
Lower Matecumbe	447
Craig	451
Long Key Fishing Camp	457
Marathon (Sombrero Lodge)	474
Pigeon Key	478
Spanish Harbor	489
Big Pine	492

(Big Pine Key is now the site of the last remaining mile post marker still in its original location, on the east side of U.S. Highway 1.)

Pirates Cove Fishing Camp	503
Perky	506
Key West	522

At this point, the astute Keys historian or FEC buff will ask, "Which were agency stations where one could purchase a ticket from a ticket agent and which were not?" Fortunately, the various timetables, through the use of bold capital letters next to the station's name, provided that information. A large "A" indicated that the station did enough business to warrant an agent; a "C" was the symbol for a "commission station," indicating that only local (on the FEC) tickets were sold and through tickets were not available at those stations. Once passengers boarded a train in the Keys with only a local ticket but with plans to continue on to a destination north or west of Jacksonville, he or she would have to detrain in Miami and purchase the through ticket

The depot at Marathon. The semaphore arms indicate that the next train will stop there.

at the depot ticket office there. An "N" indicated that the station was open twenty-four hours a day, as there were either trains arriving late at night (or departing in the wee hours) or enough business to warrant keeping the station open around the clock.

Another symbol in FEC timetables, similar to what a paragraph symbol looks like in copyediting marks, was also used, but only at one station. That symbol, with an accompanying note, told the passengers that the particular train they were on would stop for twenty minutes for refreshments at the Long Key Fishing Camp, as that was the only station between Miami and Key West with food service facilities at hand. (While Miami did have a lunch counter, the Long Key station did not. Passengers were welcome to walk down the stairs and then proceed to the fishing camp's snack bar. There was, of course, a dining room there, but passengers would not have had time to be graciously served and return to their train in time for its on-time departure.)

The February 1925 passenger timetable shows agency stations at Florida City (southernmost manned station on the mainland), Key Largo, Islamorada, Marathon and Key West, and all except Key Largo were open at night. However, the remaining twenty-five stations on the extension, other than the four below Florida City that were agency stations, were shown in the timetable with the legend "f," indicating that trains would only stop at those locations if flagged. The only stations where trains were required to stop in February 1925 were the four named above that were shown as agency stations.

By May 1935, the situation was a bit different. There were no longer any twenty-four-hour stations south of Miami, and there were no commission ticket stations; passengers were required to purchase their local tickets from the conductor on the train, and if they were going past Jacksonville, they could stop in Miami and buy their through tickets there. This was similar to the previous arrangement except that the local ticket was purchased on board from the train conductor.

In that timetable, Florida City had lost its designation as an agency station; hence, the closest agency station where tickets could be purchased was Homestead, two miles north at MP 394. The agency stations in the Keys, and the only ones where one passenger train a day in each direction was required to stop, were Islamorada (Caribee Colony), Long Key Fishing Camp, Marathon (Sombrero Lodge) and Key West, Key Largo having lost its agent and Long Key gaining one year round instead of strictly in the winter season.

It was the height of the Depression, and both freight and passenger business were at record lows, the passenger service carding one-seven-car passenger train in each direction daily, with the freight service down to a relatively short tri-weekly train in either direction. That decline in business, coupled with the fact that the railroad had been in bankruptcy since 1931 and the terrible economic situation created by the Depression, makes it easy to understand why, with the devastation wreaked by the 1935 hurricane, the FEC was in no financial position to rebuild and reopen the line.

In 2012, as the centennial of the extension is being celebrated, there are, with the exception of the structures on Pigeon Key, no known FEC buildings still in existence in the Keys, and even the Key West station, a substantial structure and the largest of the railroad's buildings in the Keys,

Although photographed after abandonment, its sign having been removed, the Big Pine Key
Depot at least provided refuge from inclement weather during its years of service. Standing in
front of the depot are O.D. Kirkman (left) and, closer to the camera, W.A. Anderson.

was demolished by the navy. The only places where one can enjoy the images
of the stations that once stood as waiting rooms along the FEC right of way
are the Bramson Archive or the several museums or libraries listed in the
acknowledgements, introduction or epilogue in this book, with a scant too
few in private hands.

As unhappy as it is that not a single building from the extension remains
in existence except on Pigeon Key, it is still a joyous occasion when one
happens upon photos, tickets or any other type of memorabilia from those
once busy, active and essential Keys structures. The photos and memorabilia
of the Key West Extension are today's link to that grand and glorious past.

8
Long Key Fishing Camp

There has been, in the books and relatively recent articles dealing with this very special place—the Long Key Fishing Camp—only the most minimal of writings.

During the life of the camp, and to no small extent because of the influence of the great American writer Zane Grey, a number of articles appeared in various magazines and newspapers, including "The Tarpon of Long Key" by Harold Roberts (*Field and Stream*, January 1913); "Life and Fun at Long Key" by Fred Bradford Ellsworth (*Outdoor Life*, February 1916); the *Key West Citizen*; the *Miami Metropolis* and the *Miami Herald*, as well as others in and outside of Florida. Once the camp was destroyed in the 1935 hurricane, with the exception of a newspaper article noting the sale of the property by the FEC Hotel Company in 1945, it was as if the camp had never existed, given the dearth of historic writing regarding that unique hostelry.

Fortunately, in *Florida Keys Magazine*'s March 1985 issue, an article by Captain Love Dean titled "Zane Grey and the Long Key Fishing Camp" appeared, but with the exception of my 1992 master's degree thesis, prepared as part of the degree requirements at Florida International University's School of Hospitality and Tourism Management and titled "Rural Hospitality in the Florida Keys: Long Key Fishing Camp 1904–1935," there seems to have been no other writing about the camp. Hopefully, this chapter will remedy that void.

Long Key Fishing Camp

This photograph is extremely important both to the railroad buff and the Keys historian in general, as it shows, along with the tents on the left and the building on the right that would become part of the fishing camp, the narrow-gauge railroad on Long Key that served as the main method of moving men and supplies the length of the island during construction. Once the work camp was converted to the fishing camp, the trackage was removed, with the exception of the short piece that took fishermen from the docks to the east side of the island via a tunnel under the main line track at the south end of the island.

What would become the internationally famed fishing resort—the FEC Hotel Company's only casual and informal inn—began its existence under totally different circumstances. In its previous incarnation, the fishing camp was the FEC's largest laborers' camp and men's quarters in the Keys. Conveniently located at milepost 458, almost exactly midway between Homestead and Key West, Long Key was the logical choice for a major campsite.

While there are no extant records indicating exactly when the decision was made to take advantage of Long Key's location and place the camp there, it is obvious that it was the prime location for such a major base of operations. Although the exact date of the establishment of the camp is unknown, we do know that, by August 1907, meals were being served to employees on a regular basis.

It is difficult to ascertain either the number of buildings that were originally used by the railroad or the number that became part of the fishing camp. While educated conjecture may serve valid purpose, problems arise when attempting to determine which buildings, following conversion, continued to be used by the railroad and which were turned over to the hotel company.

The FEC Railway's 1926–27 "Insurance List," in the files of the Bramson Archive, provide a case in point. Twelve buildings are listed as being owned by the railroad on Long Key in that report. While it is obvious that building number 1582, the passenger station, is railroad owned and located on the east (Atlantic) side of the tracks, several of the other buildings do not provide the same ease of identification in terms of photographic images. Simply put, we are unable to determine the physical location of the section foreman's cottage, the three laborers' houses, the cookhouse or the tool house. If they are on the west side of the track, we would know with almost complete certainty that the buildings in question are railroad buildings; if they are on the east (ocean) side, it will be very difficult to ascertain with the same level or degree of certainty.

Although we cannot determine the exact date of the decision to convert the labor camp to a guest-oriented fishing camp/resort, we know from announcements in FEC Railway publications of the era that "the Camp will open December 21, 1908."

That would be in line with the halting of the construction at Knight's Key Terminal in 1908, that temporary end-of-line location only nineteen miles from Long Key. With that construction hiatus and the laying off, or furloughing, of construction forces, the Long Key labor and supply camp may simply have outlived its usefulness as the main labor camp.

Given that this was likely the case, it is safe to assume that since the FEC Hotel Company had operations all along the east coast, from Atlantic Beach, near Jacksonville, south to Miami (and with two hotels in Nassau, Bahamas), the opportunity to assume responsibility for the existing Long Key facilities and convert them to use as a hospitality operation was both immediate and irresistible as the capital and acquisition costs would be comparatively minimal.

As stated above, the exact date of the decision to convert Long Key labor camp into a tourist/fishing/resort property managed by the hotel company and call it Long Key Fishing Camp is unknown, but fortunately, the *Miami*

Long Key Fishing Camp

Metropolis (predecessor of the *Miami Daily News*) carried an article on September 25, 1908, titled "Tourist Paradise to be Arranged at Long Key," which provided a good bit of information on the soon-to-be informal resort.

"News has been given out," the *Metropolis* stated,

> *that the Florida East Coast Hotel Company will soon begin to make some great improvements at Long Key, and by the beginning of the tourist season will have an attractive place arranged there for sportsmen who love to fish. At Long Key during the building of the great viaduct there were many small houses built to accommodate the workmen, and it is proposed that these buildings be gathered in one spot, making a small village.*

In terms of preciseness of dates (in comparison to the date of the company's decision to convert the labor camp) we are more fortunate regarding the opening of the fishing camp. FEC Railway passenger timetable number 77, dated January 5, 1909, advised that "the camp will open on December 21, 1908 [timetables were often put out several weeks ahead of their effective dates, hence the backdated information regarding the camp's opening] and be in charge of Mr. L.P. Schutt, and the rate will be $3.00 per day and up."

While the remainder of the FEC Hotel Company's properties were oriented to the luxury or "carriage" trade, open only in the winter season (with the singular exception of the Continental Hotel at Atlantic Beach, near Jacksonville, which was a summer-only resort), Long Key Fishing Camp patrons were advised, in the same timetable, that "they should not get the idea that this camp is luxurious in its appointment and that the table and service will be maintained on a par with the hotels of the Florida East Coast Hotel Company. It is rather a typical sub-tropical 'fishing camp,' with everything complete, sanitary and comfortable, located in the center of the famous fishing grounds of the Florida archipelago."

Dining, it was made quite clear, would be hearty, nutritious and filling, but not necessarily gourmet or elegant. "A specialty will be made of serving sea food," the timetable states, "and this alone will be enough to entice many visitors." The hotel company, in providing its copy to the railroad for use in the timetable section dedicated to the hotel company's inns, was blunt and to the point: "The table will be abundantly supplied with sea foods, fruits and vegetables properly prepared and satisfactorily served."

Following the announcement of the conversion, the *Miami Metropolis* of October 23, 1908, carried the following as the railroad and hotel company jointly announced that six buildings were being erected at Long Key for the use of tourists "and, incidentally, to allow the traveling public to stop over… and enjoy some of the best fishing in the world."

The small buildings at the former work camp were of various configurations and sizes. Though the concept was rustic, the camp was to be as attractive and inviting as possible, and the idea of using the former workmen's houses was both practical and logical.

The *Metropolis* of September 25, 1908, commented that "these houses will be made as comfortable as possible, and everything will be made as convenient as the sportsmen who are expected to go there could wish. Shower baths will be put in the houses and many other modern conveniences will be installed." The larger buildings, according to that same article, were to be erected by the company's forces, with the exception of the dining hall, which

There has never been a date established with certainty for this photo, but the fact that 4-4-0 #22 is hauling a three-car passenger train makes it almost certain that, given the still rudimentary conditions at Long Key, the line had been opened to the Knight's Key Terminal, but Long Key had not yet transitioned into the famed fishing camp it would become.

was to be converted from a quarterboat, one of several that had been used for living quarters for the workmen on the extension.

Six buildings were to be erected at Long Key, and the *Metropolis* of October 23, 1908, reported that "in the group of buildings will be four 23 x 60 feet, with a five foot veranda all around, one 90 x 23 to be used as a dining room [this apparently refers to the quarterboat noted in the previous paragraph] and one 48 x 40 feet, with a twelve foot veranda all around; a building 30 x 30 immediately in the rear will be used as a kitchen."

The setting for the camp was close to paradisiacal. The buildings, according to several FEC Railway publications, "are located in a beautiful grove of cocoanut palms on the southeastern extremity of the island overlooking a charming bay with gently shelving hard sand beach. It is accessible to boats of all sizes, has adequate harbor facilities, and is a most attractive spot. Too much can not be said in praise of the beauty of the camp and surroundings."

The *Metropolis*, in its description of the surroundings, was almost as lyrical, and in the paper's September 25, 1908 edition, the following was written:

> *Long Key has more natural beauty than most of the chain [of] keys, and the new resort or camp will be located in the midst of a beautiful grove of cocoanut trees, where one can look out on the white sand beach and across the blue waters of the ocean. It would be impossible to give a proper description of the beauty of the place but it is not too much to say that it will be one of the best patronized sportsmen's camps in the world after the visitors become acquainted with it.*

Though the prediction appeared boastful at the time, the veracity of the prognostication was to be borne out in the coming years.

The railroad and the hotel company both seemed to feel that there were not enough adjectives to truly relate to the prospective tourist or sportsman the desirability of Long Key as a destination. In their jointly issued *The East Coast of Florida*, published in October 1909 for the 1909–10 season, the publicist's glowing prose notes that "too much can not be said in praise of the beauty of the camp and its surroundings."

Once the fishing camp was opened, the routine of day-to-day operation was to begin, with one major caveat. Unlike most hospitality operations (and, certainly, those of the FEC Hotel Company), the Long Key Fishing

Camp was not accessible by road. In fact, at the time of the camp's opening, Long Key bore the distinction of having the only automobile or wagon road on the Florida Keys for the entire 156-mile distance between Miami and Key West.

The road on Long Key was a shell road, about a mile long, and wound in and around the cocoanut palms. It was deemed to be, according to an article in the *Metropolis* on May 22, 1908, "really a fine road, costing scarcely anything to build...Ocean View Drive would be a very appropriate name for this creation."

Transportation of goods, supplies and guests was almost solely by train, with a very limited amount of materiel and a minimal number of passengers arriving by boat. To the very end—the hurricane of September 2, 1935—Long Key was served almost exclusively by train.

Though roads had been built for the purpose of connecting the Keys to the mainland, there were no plans on the part of either the state or the federal government to bridge the two longest water gaps, one of 2.73 miles in length beginning at the south end of Long Key and the other, seven miles in length,

This circa 1912 view is looking north from the north end of Long Key Viaduct, with a passenger train at the station and the two-story lodge on the right. The dock master's office and boat docks are out of sight to the left, while the right of way of the narrow-gauge railway emerging from the tunnel under the main line can be seen between the second and third telephone poles on the right side of the track.

separating Knight's Key from Little Duck Key. Though automobiles and small trucks could make the journey from Miami to Key West, the amount of time required due to the poor condition and narrowness of the roads, coupled with the mandatory ferry use in two places along the route, made it almost *de rigueur* to use the train.

Extant material dealing with Long Key relates almost exclusively to the "fishing angle," with little, if anything, being written about the hospitality operation. Therefore, for what may be the first time in the history of the railroad, the hotel company, Long Key or the Florida Keys in general, it is now quite apparent that we must look at and examine the management and operation of the hospitality enterprise at Long Key Fishing Camp.

The camp operated, as did all of the other Flagler hotels (with the exception of the short-lived summer-only operation of the Continental in Atlantic Beach), exclusively in the winter season, although the boat docks were kept in service throughout the summer with a minimum of passenger train revenue being generated. Though the docks were open, the camp was closed with only the caretakers in attendance. Camp employees would generally take several weeks to "close down" before boarding FEC trains,

The scale for weighing fishermen's catches was adjacent to the dock master's office at the south end of the island.

The women in the hats standing at the dock master's office are Zane Grey's lady friends. This photo by Mr. Grey is, along with numerous others he took in Long Key and Palm Beach, in the Bramson Archive. The hatless woman on the right may be Mrs. Schutt, wife of the fishing camp's manager.

along with their compatriots at the other Flagler System hotels, and heading north for the summer, some to work at hotels in the Adirondacks, some in Maine or New Hampshire resorts and a small number at hotels in the Catskills. At the end of the summer season in the North, the process would be repeated, and the employees would return to their Florida properties for the winter season.

Unfortunately, very little regarding the hospitality end of the fishing camp's business has survived in any form, as between the destruction caused to the camp by the 1935 hurricane and the complete trashing of the hotel company's files when it closed its last office in the City Building in St. Augustine, a pitifully minimal amount of historic data relating to number of employees, yearly revenues, number of meals served, food ordered, supplies used or operating or capital expenditures is extant.

The article in *Florida Keys* magazine is indicative of the lack of attention given to the operation of the fishing camp. In her excellent four-page piece, Captain Love Dean focuses on Zane Grey and his "adventures" off-shore at Long Key but gives no indication of the details of the day-to-day operation of the club or camp.

Long Key Fishing Camp

Dean mentions that "on Long Key, Flagler built a construction camp which later became a fishing camp and a haven for notables and millionaires who arrived via rail or yacht to enjoy the outstanding fishing...For their convenience Flagler built a narrow gauge railway that ran through a tunnel under the railroad station from the Gulfside [*sic*] of the Key to the Oceanside [*sic*], where the clubhouse and guest cottages were located." Although we are fortunate that Captain Dean, in 1985, wrote the article, several of the statements related to the tunnel are incorrect.

The tunnel was built by Mr. Flagler, but not for the convenience of visitors to Long Key. Rather, it was part of the narrow-gauge railway that was put in place on Long Key to move supplies, material and workers to and from various parts of the island. Once the labor camp was closed, the narrow-gauge railroad was removed, but the tunnel was left in place; it was then used by those who wished to walk under the railroad embankment from the docks (at the south end of the island) to the fishing camp side. The tunnel was not placed under the railroad station but rather under the right of way south of the station.

In 1913, an article titled "The Tarpon of Long Key" appeared in *Field and Stream* magazine and also completely ignores daily life at the camp. Other

The depot was on the east side of the single-track main line, and passengers and employees could use either steps or a ramp to reach it. The passenger train in this image is southbound.

than mentioning the arrival at Long Key by train and "a three minute walk through the cocoanut grove…from the railroad station," no further discussion of any phase of camp life or activity appears in the article.

When staff or guests, other than business moguls or those at the highest levels of society—or famed sportsmen or writers such as Zane Grey—are mentioned, the references appear to have been, for the most part, either humorous or disparaging, unless the topic was specifically fishing. A February 1916 article in *Outdoor Life* magazine bears examples of both the humor and the deprecation. In a rare discussion of a staff member, author Fred B. Ellsworth writes:

> *A good natured colored maid…descended the stair in the main lodge carrying a heavy load of laundry on her head. "Can you carry a large load upstairs," I inquired seriously. She interpreted the meaning instantly, and, convulsed with laughter, her big black eyes sparkling and white shining teeth showing, replied, "Ah sure can, suh. If you can't carry it right up straight, so nobody can notice it, you have to carry it right off the Key. No loads am allowed at dis place."*

References made to the majority of the visitors were generally complimentary. The same article referred to "Mr. James H. Preston, the mayor of Baltimore" as "a big, handsome, suave, courtly, distinguished and highly polished gentleman," who, in the company of Mr. William Riddle, mayor of Atlantic City, "visited the camp on their way from Cuba." Yet commentary on others who were not white Anglo-Saxon could be scathing, if not blatantly anti-Semitic:

> *A caravan of Jewish people* [if Ellsworth were alive today one might be tempted to inquire as to the methods he used to determine the religion of the group he was referring to] *arrived one afternoon and were assigned the table back of me in the dining room. As anticipated, there was the continued conversation about money, diamonds, clothes and poker. Travel, science, literature, art and the absorbing topics of the time, the finer things in life, were all lost sight of, which seemed a great pity.*

What really seems a "great pity" is that Ellsworth wasted space in his article with several sentences following the above in which his blatant bigotry becomes obvious, for at no other point in the article is there any discussion of either the hospitality operation or the camp's guests.

Publicity issued by the railroad extolled the beauty of the island and the richness of the waters for fishing. In the FEC Railway's announcement booklet publicizing the opening of the Key West Extension, two sentences are the total comment dealing with the fishing camp. "Lower Matecumbe," it states, "is joined to the now well known Long Key. Here, amidst countless cocoanut trees, Long Key Camp, where fish abound and the climate is always perfect, offers a winter home for those who love an ever-changing but ever-charming sea."

A major reason for the existence of the camp was to be the fabled Long Key Fishing Club, originally founded by, among others, Zane Grey. In the 1916–17 season brochure for the fishing camp, published by the FEC Hotel Company, it is noted that Long Key has beauty, charm and mystery. An appeal was made to women to participate in the activities of the fishing club. "Women," the brochure stated, "can be comfortable, are eligible to join the club, and every inducement is offered them to take up a sport that need not mean the killing of fish."

The majority of the brochure is dedicated to discussing the fishing club and listing prizes, as well as noting, "Some of the large fish caught at Long Key during the season of 1917." Except for stating the number of guests (one hundred), the rates and the general dates of operation, no further information is provided in the brochure to enlighten the historian or hotelier regarding the hospitality operation.

In addition to the yearly brochures and booklets published by the railroad and the hotel company regarding service to company hotel properties on the east coast of Florida, the hotel company, on behalf of the fishing club, apparently issued yearly booklets listing members and the previous season's winning catches.

The 1932 booklet informs the reader that Zane Grey was president of the club from 1917 through 1919. Prominent members in 1932 included Herbert Hoover (honorary), the Countess of Suffolk, Douglas Dillon and Hamilton Wright. One member died in 1932, and five were elected to membership.

The fishing club had grown since its reorganization in 1917. According to an article in the *Key West Citizen* on March 11, 1924, titled "Long Key

An FEC Hotel Company advertisement extols the advantages of a stay at the camp. The tariff for one person in a room with a bath was seven dollars per night.

Club Elects Officers at Recent Meet," the club had 140 members and was enjoying an exceptionally successful season, being booked to capacity since early in January. Despite cool weather (for the tropical island) the popularity of the unique resort had increased remarkably. Throughout the years of its existence, numerous articles in the *Citizen* chronicled arrivals at the camp and "catches" of importance. Even in the Great Depression, the camp appeared to thrive.

Though extensive research has uncovered little in the way of concrete information regarding the day-to-day management and operation of the camp, we are able to reconstruct, using either FEC passenger timetables or the combined railway and hotel company *East Coast of Florida* booklets for each season—except for the two seasons that passed during World War I, during which the camp was apparently closed—the opening and closing dates for each season that the club operated, from 1908–09 through 1934–35.

In addition to that information, we know that the camp operated on the American plan (three meals served to guests daily) for the entire time it existed and that rates ranged from three dollars to eight or eighteen dollars per day, depending on type of room. Rates declined during the Depression and ranged from six to fifteen dollars during the later years of operation. Management of the club, during the entire life of its operation, was under

Long Key Fishing Camp

Standing on the Long Key station platform, an unknown group smiles at the camera. Since the baggage car is forward in this photo, we know that the train is southbound.

the direction of either Louis P. (L.P.) Schutt or George G. Schutt, apparently L.P.'s son.

As the Depression wore on, little changed at the camp. The trains, though fewer in number due to the decrease in business nationally, continued to stop at Long Key, and people of affluence continued to frequent the camp. Fishing remained the number one pastime, but many tourists came seeking solace and relaxation. The hotel company and the railroad—though the latter had entered receivership in 1931—continued to promote the fishing camp as a nirvana for the outdoorsman. Indeed, the passing of the years seemed only to enhance the attractiveness of Long Key.

"I have often," wrote Fred B. Ellsworth in his *Outdoor Life* article,

> *extolled the beauties and picturesqueness of this island of dreams, Long Key, and the sort of weird fascination that it possesses. There is no place in my knowledge that compares with it for such a variety of good fishing during the winter months. Many are the anglers in the north, when the winter approaches and the snow and ice mantle the earth, who begin to*

Another of Harry Wolfe's great photographs, made for the railway on June 21, 1930, shows 4-8-2 431 pulling into the Long Key depot with northbound train number 42.

dream of the Southland and prepare for departure to Long Key Fishing Camp, which generally takes place as soon as the camp opens, the latter part of December.

There one finds the blue waters of the Gulf Stream, cheerful sunshine, cloudless skies, coral beaches and pure, fresh air. The palms play gentle, sweet music and the trade winds kiss the cheeks with a fond caress, and temper the climate into an ideal one. At night the big moon and the scintillating stars smile down upon the white sands and almost turn night into day. Such is the veritable paradise for lover of rod and reel.

Sad to say, such rapturous reverie was not to continue, for the 1934–35 season would be the camp's last. On September 2, 1935, the most devastating hurricane that the western world had ever seen would destroy forty miles of track and roadbed along the Key West Extension. In one night's horrific violence, accompanied by winds strong enough to hurl men out to sea and with tidal surges vicious enough to overturn all eleven cars of the railroad's rescue train at Matecumbe, the Long Key Fishing Camp was utterly and hopelessly decimated, brutalized so completely that, along with the railroad south of Florida City, it was abandoned. The destruction was so hideous and so complete that, except for those who had known and loved the camp, no person would have known it had ever existed.

Although the hotel company was not in bankruptcy, as the railroad was, the aftermath of the hurricane was almost too shocking to comprehend (see chapter twelve). But the site of the camp and the property remained in hotel company hands until June 28, 1945, when an article in the June 29 edition of the *Key West Citizen*, headlined "Long Key Fishing Camp Brings Price of $35,000," told the story of the very end of the camp under Flagler System ownership.

"The once-famous Long Key Fishing Camp," the story reads,

> *owned and widely advertised by the Florida East Coast Hotel Company for many years, has been sold, according to a deed filed yesterday afternoon in the* [Monroe] *county clerk's office.*
>
> *The company conveyed the 45½ acre property to Scott H. Braznell of Miami for $35,000.* [In 1938, Braznell opened the hotel on Miami Beach bearing his name, advertising that it catered to a "Selected Clientele," which meant, at that time, that those of the Jewish faith "need not apply" as guests.]
>
> *No buildings are now on the site, and when it was remarked at the county court house this morning that the price was exceptionally good for unimproved property on the keys, J. Frank Roberts, chief clerk in the assessor's office, who is familiar with the topography of the keys remarked:*
>
> *I don't think it is an exceptionally good price. The former site of the fishing camp has a beautiful beach and also a good depth of water, which makes it not only an ideal spot for sport fishing, but also for commercial use. I would say the price is fair.*

Eventually, the state would buy the property in order to convert it to a state park, and with only the base of the water tank, the tunnel and the narrow-gauge wheels that once were (and may still be) on display at the park's entrance, nothing except the beautiful beaches, the magnificent moonlit nights and some of the surviving flora remains of the fabled and beloved Long Key Fishing Camp.

9
TRUMBO ISLAND TERMINAL

The story of the building and operation of the Key West Extension, possibly due to the absolute enormity of the project, the expenditure ($50 million in 1904–12 dollars) involved, the number of people associated with the task and the amount of time that has passed since the arrival of Mr. Flagler's train in 1912, has been subjected to more folderol, incorrect information, misstatements of fact and total gibberish in terms of the actual truth and realities of the project than almost any other epic of American railroad construction and operation in U.S. history. Many—if not most—of those unsubstantiated (and, often, completely false) statements seem to have come from somewhere "out of left field" and, of course, are simply not factual.

Examples run all the way from (and, yes, well before) an article in the *Miami Herald Tropic Magazine* for July 14, 1991, in which an unknown photo caption writer stated, under a picture of the eight cars of the relief train on their sides at Matecumbe following the tidal surge from the hurricane of September 2, 1935, that "the storm killed 1,000 people and toppled a train carrying 683 World War I veterans sent south to build bridges," with neither statement being true, to an article in *Key West History* in which, among other glaring errors, one story has the name of the FEC Railway shown as "Railroad" in each of its uses and the date of the railroad's entering receivership shown as 1932 although the bankruptcy was declared and actually began in 1931. Perhaps even more grievous, the name of the American Dredging Company

A general view of Trumbo Island, likely taken from the deck of one of the car ferries, circa 1927.

is shown as the "Howard Trumbo American Dredging Company," and how or where the author came up with that misnomer, only "the Shadow knows." (The actual name of the company *was* the "American Dredging Company," but never with Trumbo's name included).

That, unfortunately, is only the tip of the iceberg. In the keysnet edition of the Florida Keys *Keynoter* for July 3, 2011, the errors are rampant, ranging from a mistake in the geographic scope of the terrible freezes that occurred during the winter of 1894–95 and affected most of the state, not just West Palm Beach, to two different numbers given in two separate articles for the number of workers killed in the 1906 hurricane to the statement that the Knight's Key Dock was in the shape of a question mark (the track used to reach Knight's Key Terminal was in the shape of a question mark, not the dock itself, which was a rectangle). But wait, there's more!

A novel, even if it purports to be factual in the guise of a historic novel, is still a novel; hence, the author can be forgiven for errors under the camouflage of "literary license," but that is not so with factual tomes (or articles) that are relied upon to, and purportedly do, proffer factual information.

While it is sad indeed to consider the miscues made by so many in writing about the extension, comfort can generally be taken when examining

Martin's or Gallagher's fine works, as well as the writings of several others, and knowing that they did, indeed, "do their homework." Hopefully, that is also the case herein, and in order to discuss the construction of the FEC's Key West terminal, we must again "begin at the beginning," and that beginning is with the name Howard Trumbo.

Regretfully, other than his working for the FEC, very little has ever been uncovered on Trumbo, and numerous and repeated inquiries have turned up a minimum of information on his life, except that he was involved in various dredging and filling projects in Cuba as a contractor. A man by the name of Anders Andersen found employment with Trumbo in Cuba on a large dredging project for the Spanish-American Iron Company. What makes that important in terms of Trumbo is that Andersen returned to Florida in 1910 and, according to his memoranda, found in the FLGenWeb Digital Library and Archives, he "utilized his experience to engage in business in the employ of Mr. Trumbo as Captain at West Palm Beach…for the filling of Royal Palm Park and Floral Park at Palm Beach."

The significance of Andersen's diary, then, is clear: Was Trumbo off the job during the time that work at Key West was being held up by the navy?

4-6-2 type locomotive 121 with a passenger train on the docks at Key West. The P&O Steamship Company's *Mascotte*, formerly a Plant System boat, is at left, ready to depart for Havana.

Did he return to complete the job once the embargo was lifted and the filling operation was restarted? While those answers are unknown, that minimal tidbit of Trumbo information is more than has ever been written before, and of course, for the serious extension historian, nothing would be more satisfying than being the person who uncovers the facts regarding Trumbo's employ with the railroad and getting to "the rest of the story."

Fortunately, Tom Hambright of the Monroe Country Public Library in Key West was able to ferret out yet more information on Trumbo.

According to Hambright's diligent investigatory work, Trumbo first came to Key West in 1905 to do a major fill project for the navy. While he worked on the Key West terminal project, he also worked in Cuba. At some point, he returned to Cuba and worked there during World War I. He died there in March 1931 at the age of fifty-six. Sadly, there are no known photos of him.

Howard Trumbo was named chief engineer for the Key West terminal project—in charge of arranging for the filling in of the open water that would become that terminal—in 1906. Trumbo, in no few senses, had to be both politician and engineer, as it was necessary that he work with, appease, placate and satisfy the needs and demands of both the U.S. Navy and the U.S. Army, as well as his bosses at the FEC, including Messrs. Flagler and Parrott, and he had to work with, although not under, first James Meredith and then Bill Krome.

The Pullman sleeping car Rochambeau is in front of the camera, while, in a highly unusual scene, two P&O vessels are at the dock behind the train. Although difficult to read, it appears that the life preserver at the aft end of the ship behind the train and closest to the camera reads "Cuba," which, of course, was a P&O vessel.

A stunning view, taken by Harry Wolfe, shows the *Governor Cobb*, leased to the P&O by the New Haven Railroad–owned New England Steamship Company, awaiting its departure time. Impatient passengers on the several decks watch the proceedings on the tarmac as the last few stragglers prepare to board.

The story of the selection of what became known as Trumbo Island or Trumbo Point may have begun, according to James E. Brooks, public affairs officer for NAS Key West and a student of Key West military history, with the navy's refusal to provide land for the railroad's terminal at or near what was then called Man-of-War Harbor and is now known as Mallory Square.

Once agreement with the various military entities was reached for a railway terminal on the southwest side of the island in 1906, Trumbo began his work. Dr. Gallagher describes the challenge of the work quite succinctly in his *Florida's Great Ocean Railway*:

> *Under the direction of Howard Trumbo, a great fill area was begun in 1906, and as time progressed, this terminal area grew to 134 acres. By 1916* [the completion date of the construction of the extension], *dredging crews had moved 649,695 cubic yards of rock, over two and one-*

half million cubic yards of marl, and 6,119 cubic yards of sand and ballast to fill the terminal site and approach areas—a total of more than 3.1 million cubic yards of material—almost 18 percent of the material moved for the railway project.

The fill area became known as Trumbo's Island and was later named Trumbo Point.

Interestingly, few sources comment on the construction of the three huge docks that were built as the true "end of the line" and were the main reason for the extension and its Key West Terminal. One of those docks was seventeen hundred feet long, and the three docks must have added substantially to the total acreage of the yard.

The Havana dock was the site of the passenger station, the export dock was for receiving and shipping of general merchandise and the coal dock was built to provide storage for coal at Key West while awaiting transfer to the numerous ships then using it, rather than oil, for power.

Trumbo Island, which later became a navy seaplane base, bachelor officers' quarters and then a hostelry for visiting military personnel, as well as other military uses, was, simply put, huge, containing (as we learn from studying the two-foot by slightly more than four-and-a-half-foot FEC Railway blueprint map of the Key West Terminal) sixty-nine separate tracks. In addition to the trackage, and according to the FEC's 1926–27 "Insurance List," the terminal was the site of sixty-five separate buildings or structures, including, among others, a Pineapple Platform shed, toilets, fuel tanks, a woodworking machine shop, a wrecker shed (to house the 150-ton wrecking crane assigned to Key West), a bridge tender's house (for the bridge tender who worked the Garrison Bight Bridge), a passenger station, several freight houses, a stock pen, storerooms and much more.

The "Insurance List" is of immeasurable value, as not only does it list each building, but it also states the building number (every FEC building had and has a number for insurance and identification purposes) and the value of the building and its contents. The aforementioned map not only shows each building on the site but also provides its number so that the location on the grounds can be matched to the insurance list.

Passenger trains and locomotives arriving in Key West had to be turned for the northbound trip, and since the Key West terminal had neither a loop

With the station to the left, and the Western Union and Bell Telephone signs prominent on the roof, a large crowd waits to board a northbound train at Key West.

nor a turntable for the locomotives, a wye had to be built. The wye left the yard toward its south end and ended in the city itself, at Francis and Eaton Streets. The wye was long enough so that the trains, after arriving at the passenger station, could be backed on to the south leg of the wye and then pulled forward on the north leg back into the yard. In the center of the wye were the stock pen and the freight house, both, of course, accessible to and facing the mainline track.

Another interesting part of the Key West operation was the track that left the north leg of the wye, crossed the south leg and went into Key West, the total length of that track being 1,667 feet. That track crossed Grinnell Street and ended about 150 feet south of Grinnell, parallel to Caroline Street. There were two sidings that came off the main spur track, both of which ended on the north side of Grinnell. Those tracks were likely used as what are called "team" tracks and are where freight cars could be spotted

There are just too many incredible Harry Wolfe photos to claim one as "the best," but for Key West images, this marvelous view of 4-8-2 431 (also shown previously at Long Key Depot) with a train of water tank cars must rank very close to "the top."

for loading or unloading by local businesses, although one of the tracks, according to Steve Strunk, served a meatpacking plant.

No discussion of Trumbo can or would be complete without a look at the car ferry service, the "Florida-Havana All-Rail Route," which began operating between the ferry dock at Trumbo Island and the Havana terminal in 1915. It should—it must—be noted that at no time in the history of the car ferry operation were passenger cars brought aboard the ferries, as they were strictly used for the freight operation. Passengers were welcome to detrain from the various FEC passenger trains and walk the short distance across the tarmac to the welcoming gangplank of whichever P&O steamship was awaiting them for the short, ninety-mile journey across the Straits of Florida to "gay Havana."

I would be remiss if I did not warmly acknowledge Florida East Coast Railway Society president Calvin Winter, who, in the May 2011 issue of

Although the date of this photo of the Key West Depot is unknown, it appears that, given the automobiles in the left background, this picture was taken in the late teens or very early 1920s.

Speedway, the official publication of the society, wrote a marvelous article on the history of the car ferry operation, and much of what is below in terms of information on the car ferries is taken from Calvin's article.

The FEC first established railroad car ferry service from Key West to Havana in 1915, using three virtually identical car ferries very similar to those used by railroads such as the Grand Trunk Western, Ann Arbor and Pere Marquette in their Lake Michigan services. The boats were built by William Cramp & Son of Philadelphia and named *Henry M. Flagler*, *Joseph R. Parrott* and *Estrada Palma*. (Tomas Estrada Palma was president of Cuba from 1902 through 1906, the first president of the Cuban republic following the Spanish-American War.)

Each of the boats had four tracks and could carry twenty-eight forty-foot freight cars. The United Railways of Havana and Western Railways of Havana provided connecting Cuban rail service for freight cars moving to and from the island nation. Although the railroad formed a separate company to manage and operate the car ferry service (Florida East Coast Car Ferry Company), the Interstate Commerce Commission, in another of its brutally nonsensical, thoughtless, anti-competitive and prejudiced-against-a-railroad decisions, decided that the car ferry company was subject

116

to its jurisdiction, while allowing other rail car ferry lines emanating from the ports of Hoboken, New Jersey, and New Orleans to go unregulated.

One of the major causes of the abandonment of the extension, according to the research done by Mr. Winter, was the loss of business to unregulated competition.

Following the '35 hurricane, the operation was moved to Port Everglades, but with the coming of World War II, the U.S. government requisitioned the boats for service as mine layers or LSTs. Following the war, the Port of Palm Beach–based West India Fruit and Steamship Company purchased the *Flagler* and the *Parrott*, and with the *Grand Haven*, which it had purchased from the Grand Trunk Western Railway in 1945, took over and made a major success of the Florida–Havana railroad car ferry service, unregulated as it

Pictured previously, W.A. Anderson (left) and O.D. Kirkman (right) stand on the dock at Key West with milepost 522, which was across from the station, in a photo taken on August 25, 1938, three years after the abandonment.

was by the ICC. (The *Estrada Palma* was severely damaged in World War II and was stripped and scrapped by the navy following the war.)

All usable material was removed from the Trumbo Island terminal yard, and as soon as the final decision was made in 1936 to end service just south of milepost 396 in Florida City and abandon the extension south of that point, the massive task of dismantling the car ferry apron and float bridge began.

The car ferries were used to move a great deal of the material from the terminal and yard, including the apron and the float bridge itself, those being relocated to Port Everglades in Fort Lauderdale in order that the car ferry service to Cuba could resume. It is apparent that the steam locomotives and other rail equipment in Key West were moved on rails to the point where the "shoo-fly" (temporary) track was put in place on Matecumbe Key for the purpose of moving steam locomotive 447 and the cars that had been overturned by the storm surge back to Miami.

Because Port Everglades could not be used as a car ferry terminal until the float bridge and apron were moved, it is quite unlikely that the rolling stock was returned to the mainland by car ferry. (Once the float bridge and apron were removed from Key West, there would have been no way to load locomotives or rolling stock on the car ferries; hence, the equipment would have had to have been brought back to the mainland by rail, over the Keys, using the temporary track.)

While, hopefully, some long-lost documentation may turn up, it appears to be quite logical that, following the loading of the car ferry apron and float bridge onto the ferry, the big wrecking crane, and all passenger and freight cars still in the Key West yard would have had to have been pulled out by locomotive. While photos exist of the shoo-fly track in place, it appears that, with no apron or float bridge at Key West, the only way to have moved the rolling stock and equipment would have been by one or more special trains to the point where the damaged trackage had been temporarily reinstalled.

Once the very last train (so, it appears, the "last train *to* paradise" was actually the last train *from* paradise, and it was a train of equipment, not passengers) had passed over the forty-mile stretch that had been damaged in the storm and rebuilt only temporarily to allow the movement of the last of the FEC's equipment from Key West, it is safe to hypothesize that the track, along with all other FEC trackage in the Keys, was either removed or, in the

Trumbo Island Terminal

Following the abandonment and subsequent purchase by the navy, the FEC yard was completely transformed, until, finally, the only original building on the site was the former passenger station. It is shown here as the "Naval Ordnance Unit" and later became the personnel section, finally being torn down by the navy, circa 1997.

cases of the rails on several of the bridges, used as side or guard rails when the highway was built.

In either 1937 or 1938, the navy purchased Trumbo Island from the FEC for $800,000, following the state's purchase of the right of way in 1936 for $640,000, so what had cost Mr. Flagler $50 million between 1904 and 1912 was sold to two government entities at the height of the Great Depression for $1,640,000, one of the greatest deals ever engineered by government or private enterprise in the history of America.

10

DAILY OPERATIONS

As much as we would like to attach an unending aura of romance to the operation of the trains, stations and other railway facilities in and on the Keys, the truth of the matter is that, just like railroading in the high Sierras or the Colorado Rockies, or through the Cascade Mountains, the views, scenes and vistas may be interesting, unique, enthralling and perhaps even exciting the first several times, but after that, they become what we can only refer to as "routine."

There is no question that the trips by Mr. Krome and the engineering staff and Mr. Flagler and his invited guests on January 21 and January 22, 1912, were "magical," but within just a few days, operating the railroad that went to sea was, as noted above, "routine." And while it may at first seem almost blasphemous to use that term, all one needs to do is to think of or about airline pilots, most of whom, while enjoying their work, will not hesitate to tell any who may ask that, indeed, it is rather repetitive, and they have been trained (hopefully carefully) to do their jobs to the best of their ability. That was all that could be asked of those who worked on the extension, from the superintendent (the chief operating officer of the division) to his assistants, to the train and station crews and employees, to the mechanical people who worked at their various tasks relating to the extension from Miami to Key West or, in the case of the car ferry employees or the P&O Steamship Company people, from Key West to Havana.

With the foreman standing at right, eight men are busy doing maintenance work, an absolute necessity every single day of railroad operation. *Courtesy HistoryMiami.*

To most of them, it was "a job," and that was their livelihood. They did their jobs, and they did them well, but the reader should understand that when one performs the same task or tasks (generally speaking) on a continuous basis, the job can almost be done by rote.

Essentially, beginning on January 22, 1912, and continuing through the morning of September 2, 1935, the professionals did their jobs on a daily basis and did them efficiently and effectively, many remaining with the railroad and at those jobs (or, in some cases, attaining promotions) for a number of years.

Daily operations began, as noted, on January 22, 1912, with FEC passenger timetable number 91. South of Homestead, beginning on that day, there were twenty-five stations served by two passenger trains daily, plus one freight train, which would pick up and drop off at any station where there was a load to be delivered or accepted for shipment. As noted previously, several of the stations had names but no facility of any kind, and those are shown in the timetable, along with most of the stations that did have a physical structure, as flag stops.

Southbound, combined trains 87, the all-Pullman sleeping car Atlantic Coast Line-FEC New York and Florida Special, and 99, the also all-Pullman Seaboard Florida Limited, made only two stops between Miami and Key West (and, conversely, northbound), those being at Long Key and Marathon, with a point-to-point operating time of exactly six hours. Trains 37 and 38 did not operate in the same manner.

			No.	Station			
5.00	4.48	1.40	299	Lv..A.........West Palm Beach.........N.. Ar	12.35	10.07	12.30
f 5.13	5.01	f 1.50	306	Ar..A.........Lake Worth.........Lv	f12.21	9.56	f12.16
.....	f 5.06	.....	309	Ar.........Hypoluxo.........Lv		f 9.49	.....
.....	f 5.10	f 1.58	312	Ar..A.........Boynton.........Lv	f12.13	9.46	.....
5.30	5.17	f 2.04	317	Ar..A.........Delray Beach.........Lv	f12.08	9.38	f12.01
.....	f 5.22	.....	321	Ar.........Yamato.........Lv		f 9.30	.....
.....	f 5.27	f 2.14	325	Ar.........Boca Raton.........Lv	f11.58	f 9.24	.....
.....	f 5.31	f 2.19	327	Ar..A.........Deerfield.........Lv	f11.55	f 9.20	.....
f 5.52	f 5.40	f 2.28	333	Ar..A.........Pompano.........Lv	f11.48	9.12	f11.39
.....	f 5.45	.....	337	Ar.........Oakland Park.........Lv		f 9.07	.....
6.03	5.50	2.38	341	Ar..A...(Note 9).Fort Lauderdale.........Lv	11.38	9.02	11.29
.....	f 5.58	.....	346	Ar..A.........Dania.........Lv		8.51	.....
6.18	6.03	2.51	348	Ar..A.........Hollywood.........Lv	11.26	8.47	11.16
.....	f 6.08	.....	351	Ar.........Hallandale.........Lv		f 8.43	.....
.....	f 6.13	.....	353	Ar..A.........Ojus.........Lv		8.40	.....
.....	f 6.15	.....	355	Ar.........North Miami Beach.........Lv		f 8.37	.....
.....	f 6.19	.....	357	Ar.........North Miami.........Lv		f 8.35	.....
.....	f 6.26	.....	361	Ar.........Little River.........Lv		f 8.31	.....
a6.50	6.45	3.30	366	Ar..A.........Miami.........N.. Lv	11.00	8 20	b10.50
7.20 PM	PM	PM	366	Lv..A.........Miami.........N.. Ar	AM	AM	10.20
7.31			371	Ar..A.........Coconut Grove.........Lv			9.56
7.37			374	Ar.........South Miami.........Lv			9.48
f 7.42			380	Ar.........Kendal.........Lv			f 9.42
f 7.51			382	Ar..A.........Perrine.........Lv			9.33
f 7.59			386	Ar..A.........Goulds.........Lv			f 9.23
f 8.04			388	Ar..A.........Princeton.........Lv			f 9.17
f 8.09			389	Ar.........Naranja.........Lv			f 9.11
f 8.14			392	Ar.........Modello.........Lv			f 9.05
8.22			394	Ar..A.........Homestead.........Lv			9.00
f 8.27			396	Ar.........Florida City.........Lv			f 8.50
f 8.43			408	Ar.........Glades.........Lv			f 8.34
f 8.53			415	Ar.........Jewfish.........Lv			f 8.25
f 8.58			417	Ar.........Key Largo.........Lv			f 8.22
f 9.06			424	Ar.........Rockharbor.........Lv			f 8.09
f 9.16			431	Ar.........Tavernier.........Lv			f 7.59
f 9.21			434	Ar.........Plantation.........Lv			f 7.54
9.30			440	Ar..A..Islamorada (Caribbee Colony).........Lv			7.45
f 9.48			447	Ar.........Lower Matecumbe.........Lv			f 7.29
f 9.50			451	Ar.........Craig.........Lv			f 7.25
f10.01			457	Ar..A...Long Key Fishing Camp.........Lv			f 7.14
10.27			474	Ar..A...Marathon (Sombrero Lodge).........Lv			6.52
f10.35			478	Ar.........Pigeon Key.........Lv			f 6.40
f10.55			489	Ar.........Spanish Harbor.........Lv			f 6.23
f11.00			492	Ar.........Big Pine.........Lv			f 6.18
f11.15			503	Ar.........Pirates Cove Fishing Camp.........Lv			f 6.05
f11.21			506	Ar.........Perky.........Lv			f 6.00
11.50 AM			522	Ar..A.........Key West.........Lv			5.40 PM

				PENINSULAR & OCCIDENTAL S.S. CO.			
PM				Lv.........Key West.........Ar			PM
c12.20							d 3.15
c 6.20 PM				Ar.........Havana.........Lv			d 9.00 AM

				PAN AMERICAN AIRWAYS			
AM				Lv.........Miami.........Ar			PM
8.00							5.00
10.15 AM				Ar.........Havana.........Lv			2.45 PM

A true look at day-to-day operations can be garnered by using the May 18, 1935 passenger timetable, showing all stations on the extension with the arrival and departure times of the two scheduled daily trains, 75 southbound and 76 northbound, the famed Havana Special.

Daily Operations

A fireman's side view from above Pigeon Key, looking south toward Moser Channel Bridge. The track was completely elevated above this tiny island.

Trains 37 and 38 are shown as the Key West Express, which was essentially a local train between Jacksonville and Key West, carrying baggage, mail and express cars, a daily "colored coach," a Pullman buffet parlor car and other accommodations. These trains ran during the daylight hours and would have given passengers the opportunity to enjoy the Keys, the ocean and the gulf in their full glory. The two trains had required station stops at Jewfish, Central Supply, Long Key and Marathon, with all other stations shown as flag stops; hence, the scheduled trip from Key West to Miami was shown as six and a half hours (of course, that assumes that there were not too many flag stops).

By August 1912, the expected summer schedule adjustment had been made. In the winter season, all-Pullman trains were no longer operating, while trains 35 and 36 made the complete trip to and from Jacksonville. Train 23 operated south from Homestead on Tuesday, Thursday and Saturday, taking a leisurely ten daylight hours for the trip. Counterpart train 24 ran north from Key West to Homestead on Monday, Wednesday and Friday but took only eight hours and fifteen minutes for the northbound trip, which was also in the daylight.

In showing the changing operation on a day-to-day basis, the purpose is not to describe in detail how each timetable was slightly different from its predecessor but rather to give an idea of those changes at various points through the years; hence, a look at timecard 113 for January 4, 1916, will illustrate what occurred in the first four years of operation.

By that date, two trains were again making the complete trip. Trains 85 and 86, the Oversea Limited, were almost completely sleeping car trains but carried "two first class coaches for white and colored." Both the Atlantic Coast Line and the Seaboard Air Line ran from New York, along with a baggage car, a dining car that originated in Washington, D.C., a Jacksonville–Key West sleeper and a Palm Beach–Key West sleeper. That train was an overnight train in both directions between Miami and Key West. The second train, numbers 38 and 39, the Key West Express, operated between Jacksonville and Key West with the Miami–Key West portion of the trip in daylight in both directions.

Yet another four-year jump to timecard 129, dated March 10, 1920, shows two famous trains running to Key West, one of which, the Seaboard Florida Limited, would only run on the FEC until the Seaboard completed its line to West Palm Beach in 1924, while the other train, the Havana Special, would

Operating seven days a week year round, and carrying coaches, a parlor car, Pullman sleeping cars, a dining car, mail and baggage cars and an open-end observation car on the rear of the train, the famous Havana Special, shown here on Matecumbe Key, not only became completely identified with the oversea railroad's operation but also retained its name until early 1961, long after passenger service south of Miami had ended.

lose that name in 1961, becoming the East Coast Special, the name change due to Fidel Castro's takeover of Cuba in 1960.

Timecard (or timetable) 129 indicates that the all-Pullman Seaboard Florida Limited would leave Key West at 9:30 a.m. and was scheduled for required station stops at Long Key, with twenty minutes allowed for passengers to leave the train and enjoy refreshments at the fishing camp, at Islamorada and at, for some reason, Everglade (later called "Glades"), a station without a building or facility of any kind. Arrival in Miami was scheduled for 2:30 p.m., which was a five-hour trip, although every other station shown was listed as a flag stop. The southbound counterpart train left Miami at 12:01 p.m. and arrived in Key West at 6:20 p.m. with the same stops.

The Havana Special, shown as trains 85 and 86 (on the FEC southbound, numbers are and always have been odd, while northbound numbers are even) left Miami at 5:00 a.m. and arrived in Key West at 10:50 a.m. en route from New York, so early risers could see the sunrise on the left (east) side of the train as they headed south. Northbound train 86 left Havana at 8:30 p.m. and arrived Miami at 2:15 a.m.

At this point, it should be noted that all passenger trains to Key West carried baggage cars, express cars and, in many cases, railway post offices (RPOs) that would accept and deliver mail en route while sorting and cancelling the mail going to on-line stations or, if northbound, to points north of Jacksonville. The southbound trains sorted mail going on to Cuba via the P&O Steamship Co. boats awaiting the arrival of the trains in Key West or coming into Key West to connect with northbound departures.

The clerks on the RPOs carried cancellation devices quite unlike the usual post office postmarkers; their devices bore the legend (depending on the year) either Jack & Key West RPO SD (for Southern Division, which operated from Fort Pierce to Key West) or Fort Pierce & Key West RPO. Each postmarker bore the date as well as the train number, and a highly desirable collectable in the railroad or RPO collecting field is a cancellation from the RPOs serving Key West.

Due to the fact that most of the stations were flag stops, it appears that the RPOs would drop or pick up their mail pouches at the designated station stops, and a post office employee would deliver or pick up mail at the intermediate (flag) stations for delivery to the RPO clerks at the station stops. Apparently, the same process was in effect for American Railway Express

FLORIDA **EAST COAST** RAILWAY

PASS Mrs. G.Williams---colored-

FROM Jacksonville-TO Miami-

ACCOUNT Fam.emp.K.W.Ext-

ISSUED Dec 31'06 EXPIRES Jan 31'07

STOP-OVER PERMITTED AT INTERMEDIATE STATIONS

No. P 3333

VICE-PRES'T AND GEN'L MANAGER

Employees were permitted to ride FEC trains when off duty, provided they had the proper credentials and a trip or annual pass. While this pass was good during 1907 between Jacksonville and Miami, it is unique in that it was issued to a family member of a Key West Extension employee who, as may be noted, was "colored."

(later Railway Express Agency) packages and parcels, as it certainly would not have been efficient for that company to maintain agencies at any but the required station stops.

By February 13, 1925, even though the train numbers remained the same, several interesting operating changes are noted: trains 37 and 38 were both daylight runs, and both carried coaches plus a twenty-five-seat parlor car complete with a drawing room and an observation platform at the end of the car. No dining car service is shown, but the symbol next to Long Key again denotes a twenty-minute stop for refreshments.

The Havana Special continued as an overnight train in both directions. Considered a high-grade train, the consist in the timetable shows "Dining Car Service," but there is no specific designation for a dining car shown in the list of equipment. It is possible that the dining car on 85 and 86 served dinner out of Key West at 7:30 p.m. northbound and a light breakfast into Key West, with the crew quite possibly boarding at Miami for the 5:00 a.m. departure so that breakfast could be served prior to arrival in Key West at 9:30 a.m.

Service through the years of the great Florida boom of the 1920s remained fairly constant, but with the five terrible events of 1926, culminating with the September 17 and 18, 1926 hurricane that devastated Greater Miami and

A "rarer than hen's teeth" brochure, this "Going to Sea by Rail" three-fold, four-panel flyer was issued to promote service during the 1934–35 season and, with photos by Harry M. Wolfe, featured "The Most Unique Train Trip You Have Ever Taken," ballyhooing Miami–Key West round-trip excursions with a six-day limit for $4.75. For those wanting to spend one night in Key West, the "leave Miami on a Sunday and return on Monday" round-trip fare was $2.50.

killed more than four hundred people, business began to decline, slowly at first but then accelerating to and through that bleak day in October 1929 when the stock market crashed. In retrospect, and as most historians of the era now concur, the "bust" of that great Florida boom was the harbinger of the Great Depression, and that brutal financial debacle had its beginning in September 1926 in Miami.

Time table number three (the numbering system had been changed in the late 1920s, and the timetables, instead of being numbered consecutively, were numbered for each year in the order of publication) for December 2, 1930, reflected the decline in business. There were still two passenger trains to and from Key West, but one, numbers 41 and 42, which was a daylight train in both directions named the Oversea, carried coaches only and made a half-hour meal stop at Long Key Fishing Camp southbound only, while that same station was nothing more than a flag stop for the northbound train. The other train was the Havana Special; its numbers changed to 75 and 76 and would remain thus until the end of passenger service on the FEC.

The Havana Special, having overnighted from Jacksonville, left Miami at 7:15 a.m., arriving in Key West at 11:15 a.m. with no scheduled stops and only three flag stops (meaning the train would not stop at any other station),

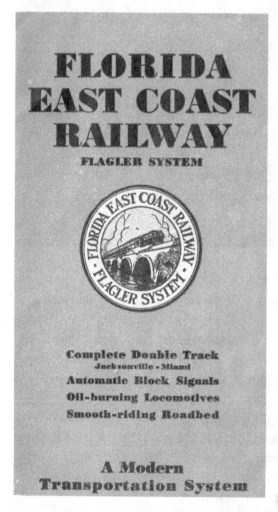

FLORIDA
EAST COAST
RAILWAY
FLAGLER SYSTEM

Complete Double Track
Jacksonville - Miami
Automatic Block Signals
Oil-burning Locomotives
Smooth-riding Roadbed

A Modern
Transportation System

Everything the railroad issued, almost from the time of its opening until 1936, featured the Key West Extension. A ticket jacket, shown here, is a perfect example of the prominence of the emblem on all FEC-published material, from stationery to timetables, matchbooks, brochures and most of the company's dining car menus of the era.

those being Homestead, Long Key Fishing Camp and Pirates Cove Fishing Camp. Obviously, breakfast on board would have been a must! Besides the few coaches and the several sleeper cars, the train carried a rear-end parlor/observation car from Miami to Key West.

The return for that train had it departing Key West at 5:30 p.m. and arriving in Miami at 9:30 p.m., with departure from there at 10:00 p.m. This was the same schedule out of Miami that the train used until January 22, 1963.

Along with all other business on the FEC and in the country in general, passenger revenues continued to decline until, with the last pre-September 2, 1935 hurricane timetable, dated May 18, 1935, only one train—the Havana Special—remained to give passenger, mail and express service to the Keys.

With a schedule essentially the same as it was in 1930, the main changes were in the equipment, with the parlor/observation car no longer in service and the dining car operating only four days a week. Most pictures of the train taken in that last season show it with seven cars behind the steam locomotive: one baggage car, one express car, one railway post office, two coaches, a sleeping car that operated only two days a week and a lounge car and dining car, each operating four days weekly.

By that time, the three manned stations were Miami, Homestead and Key West, the agents having been removed from the few others that had been agency stations.

At this point, the astute reader may ask about the operation of freight trains, as so far in this chapter only passenger trains have been discussed. Indeed, this chapter, to be complete, must include the freight train operation.

For the great majority of the life of the extension, there was one freight train scheduled each day, each way, except at the very end of service, when there was one freight train each way four times a week. Local freight number 230 would leave Key West northbound on a daily basis, going on to Kendal (spelled with one "l" in those days) and then to Hialeah Yard. The southbound train, number 343, lyrically named the Steamer Dispatch, left Hialeah at 5:00 a.m., Kendal at 5:30 a.m. and was scheduled to arrive in Key West at 11:40 a.m. The times shown in Southern Division employee timetable five for December 17, 1931, are the times that the trains were scheduled to pass each station, but as freight trains, they did not stop for passengers.

Freight trains were a major part of the Key West Extension's operation. Those trains, which carried freight cars for Cuba, connected on a daily basis with the FEC Car Ferry Company's giant car ferries. The *Henry M. Flagler*, shown here, carried twenty-eight loaded freight cars.

Through the employee (also known as the "working" or "operating" timetables, which are for the use of employees only) timetables, we learn several interesting facts about the operation of the extension.

Key West was home to at least three FEC "local surgeons," the term then in use for physicians; U.S. Army litter number twelve was kept at Key West; one of the division's six stock pens was at Key West, the location mentioned in the previous chapter; after leaving Homestead there were water tanks (for locomotives to refill) at Glades, Islamorada, Marathon, Cudjoe and Key West; and Frank Johnson was the local watch inspector in Key West.

As part of what are termed "Fifth District Special Instructions," the following information regarding the operation on the Keys is given: the maximum gross weight of car and lading allowed from Miami to Key West was 210,000 pounds; there were no crossovers south of Miami; there was a standard time clock at the Key West telegraph office; Key West was a station with a train register book (the engineer and conductor of every train had to register upon arrival or before departure); the speed of trains on the three longest Keys bridges ranged from ten to twenty-five miles per hour; the speed at which trains were allowed to pass over drawbridges at Jewfish,

Moser Channel, Channel Five and Key West was four miles per hour; and, finally, seven-hundred- and eight-hundred-class engines and four-hundred-class engines double heading were limited to twenty miles per hour over the Tavernier Creek, Snake Creek and Bahia Honda Bridges.

Because there were no electric light signals on the line south of Miami, all train operation was governed by train orders, prepared at stations at which there was an agent/telegrapher and either handed to the train crews or passed up to them with the train in motion via a train order hoop. Because the agency stations were so few and far between, and with no electric light signals, train crews were constantly warned about the issues regarding, and the need for, unending caution and safety.

Was working on the Key West Extension exciting? Probably for a short time, but exciting or not, the employees knew then—and we know now—that they were participating in and contributing to the greatest and most incredible railroad ever built in America and, quite possibly up to that time, the world.

11

THE CASA MARINA

For many, many years, most FEC buffs have believed that the beautiful Casa Marina Hotel (the "House by the Sea"), which opened with a glorious dinner and ball on New Year's Eve 1920, was the Flagler System's first hospitality endeavor in Key West itself. That was not the case.

From 1897 until either late 1900 or early 1901, the FEC Hotel Company either owned or leased the Key West Hotel, which showed up in the joint FEC Railway and Hotel Company's *East Coast of Florida* booklets for those four years but disappeared from the folders thereafter. From then until 1920, the FEC Hotel Company did not have a Key West property.

The Hotel Key West is somewhat of an FEC mystery. While the company's publications from the years noted above recognize the hotel as part of the hotel company's system, there is, unlike from any of the other FEC hotels, no extant information or memorabilia known to exist from the hotel.

Incredible as it may at first seem, there is no mention of the hotel in any of the three Flagler biographies. The mystery is compounded when what is still considered to be the best history of Key West, Jefferson B. Browne's *Key West: The Old and the New*, published in 1909, contains nary a word on or about the hotel. None of the usual Key West historic sources, whether institutional or private, could provide any information on the hotel's operation, including longtime Keys residents and historians Phyllis and Steve Strunk.

The Casa Marina

The Casa Marina's predecessor in terms of an FEC Hotel Company hostelry in Key West was the hotel named for its city. When it was sold, the name was changed to the Jefferson, and that hotel, née the Key West, is shown in this 1910 view.

What *is* known about the Hotel Key West is that it was acquired by the hotel company in, apparently, late 1897, the property having first opened, according to the information in the FEC Hotel Company's 1897–98 advertising booklet for the system, in February of 1897. The manager was Leon H. Cilley, and his name, after appearing in that season's booklet, is never seen again or further associated with any FEC hotels. For the remainder of the hotel's life as an FEC hotel, its manager was G. Butler Smith. Smith, like Cilley, would disappear from the company's history once the FEC gave up its operation of the hotel, apparently following the 1900–1901 season.

The Hotel Key West would eventually become known as the Jefferson Hotel following its life as an FEC property. Once the hotel was relinquished by the FEC Hotel Company, there would not be another FEC hotel presence in Key West until the breaking of ground for the Casa Marina in late 1918, although it should be noted that planning for the Casa Marina actually began in 1914, two years after Mr. Flagler died, but was interrupted by the necessity of the company focusing its attention on the problems and issues brought about by World War I.

CASA MARINA

KEY WEST, FLORIDA

Most uniform and delightful Climate in America

Opens December 30th, 1922, Closes March 31st, 1923

RATES:

Single room with private bath . .	$ 9.00	per day
Two single rooms with private bath .	16.00	" "
Double room with private bath (twin beds)	16.00	" "
Double and single rooms with private bath for three persons	24.00	" "

We have a few rooms without bath at $6.00 to $7.00 per day per person.

OPERATED ON AMERICAN PLAN ENTIRELY

Casa Marina
Key West, Florida

© MAJOR HAMILTON MAXWELL

THE latest of the Florida East Coast Hotel Company's (Flagler System) chain of resort hotels, picturesquely located on the South Shore overlooking the waters of the Florida Straits; giving and unusual sea view. New pier for yachts and fishermen, ocean bathing, miniature golf course on grounds (9 holes), A-1 tennis courts. Climate the most uniform in America. Seasons 1920-21 and 1921-22 (December to May) mercury was not below 60° nor above 80° Fahrenheit at Casa Marina. The fishing in Key West waters is equal to any.

RATES (American Plan entirely)

OPEN UNTIL MARCH 31st 1 9 2 3	SINGLE ROOM WITH PRIVATE BATH, $9.00 PER DAY DOUBLE ROOM WITH PRIVATE BATH, $16.00 PER DAY A FEW ROOMS WITHOUT PRIVATE BATH, $6 & $7 PER DAY ALL OUTSIDE ROOMS	L. P. SCHUTT MANAGER

This page: The 1922–23 season Casa Marina rate card (December 30, 1922–March 31, 1923) notes that single rooms with private baths were nine dollars per night, with other rates also noted. The hotel operated on the three-meals-per-day American plan. For that same season, manager L.P. Schutt issued this promotional postcard extolling the sports opportunities and the weather.

A very rare look at the Casa's lobby, which featured rattan chairs with flowered cushions, armchairs toward the rear and even a smoking stand for the use of those addicted to the demon tobacco.

Unfortunately, as with so many other areas of or parts of the FEC Railway and/or the hotel company in dealing with the history of the extension, much of what has been written on and about the Casa Marina is incorrect.

Following the completion of the railway to Key West, the hotel company's management pondered the validity and value of establishing a property at "the end of the line." Results from Long Key Fishing Camp had been excellent and well above expectations, but Key West called for a full-service and full-facility hotel, along the lines of the company's other hotels with the exception of the fishing camp.

The initial approach was to attempt to predict occupancy rates through patronage on the oversea extension. If, as Mr. Flagler believed prior to his death in 1913, the extension would produce full passenger train loads, or at least was capable of doing so, then the potential for a full-service facility hotel in Key West was worth considering. The railroad-provided statistics encouraged the hotel company and led it to believe that there was great potential in building a Key West property.

Although travel to the island city was increasing almost monthly, World War I, as noted above, intervened. Once the company was given the approval by the War Department, though, planning continued, and ground was broken late in 1918.

Designed and built to take advantage of both the view and the ocean breezes, Casa Marina—the house by the sea—positioned itself as the ideal location for both business and pleasure. The 1921 Hotel Company's Casa Marina brochure stated that the hotel was "the ideal location for several days of relaxation or refreshment before proceeding with your busy schedule en route to or from Cuba."

Indeed, the location facing the Atlantic Ocean was a delight. By its third season (1922–23) the hotel, in an advertising postcard issued that season, stated that the climate was the most uniform in America and that during the seasons of 1920–21 and 1921–22 ("season" equates to late December through early May), the mercury was neither below sixty degrees nor above eighty degrees Fahrenheit at Casa Marina.

Construction material rolled in unhindered on the oversea railway, and with World War I coming to a close, the pace of construction was intensified. In a March 31, 1992 conversation, historian and author Phyllis Strunk stated that "the Casa Marina was built of poured concrete and steel reinforcements, and was virtually hurricane-proof."

The hotel opened with a gala New Year's Eve ball on December 31, 1920, which continued on and into Saturday, January 1, 1921. Longtime Long Key Fishing Camp manager Louis P. Schutt oversaw every detail of the building of the hotel (of which he was scheduled to become manager), as well as making certain that every facet of the brand-new hotel was at its best for the grand opening ball. Many Key Westers, according to a story on page one of the Key West *Citizen's* January 21, 1921 edition, said that the opening was "the biggest party Key West has had since the opening of the Key West Extension."

The Casa Marina was the first truly first-class hotel that Key West had seen. The company located the hotel on the beach facing the gulf at the west end of the island, and the property included ample grounds that were planned for development into "a real tropical garden with a variety of plants not to be found at any other point on the mainland."

The building itself was built in the Spanish Renaissance style, with fireproof roofs, extensive loggias and a pavilion design, in order that every room was an outside room. The hotel was built with enormous rooftop cisterns to collect rain to provide fresh water, but if the rains were not

The Casa Marina

The beauty of the hotel is evidenced by its stunningly verdant gardens.

forthcoming, the hotel simply tapped into its cross-island connections with the massive water tanks at the FEC terminal at Trumbo Island. Those tanks, incidentally, were supplied by regular trains of tank cars, brought down from the giant FEC pumping station at Homestead.

In later years, the hotel company advertised the hotel not only for its location as a stopping point en route to and from Cuba but also for its resort angle and its big game fishing opportunities. On-premise sports were yet another draw.

According to the hotel company's undated but circa 1938 descriptive booklet titled *The Pioneers*, "The waters around Key West and adjacent keys afford the finest fishing grounds in the United States, which annually attract noted sportsmen...Boats and experienced guides are available at the Casa Marina docks. In addition to the thrills of big game fishing," the booklet adds, "guests at the Casa Marina enjoy excellent tennis courts and putting greens."

The hotel was opened on the American plan for dining, with three full meals per day included in the room rates, a feature that was retained until the property was sold to the U.S. government at the beginning of World War II. With an initial 175 rooms, the hotel could accommodate three hundred guests at rates that, even for the era, were far from inexpensive.

An aerial view of the hotel gives one a feeling not only for its size but also for its superb location and stunning beachfront. Key West stretches out behind the hotel.

For the opening 1921 season, guests paid from five to six dollars per day for "a few rooms without private baths" to fifteen dollars per day for double rooms with private baths. Single rooms with baths were eight dollars per day.

Rates continued to increase as the country experienced the "great boom" of the 1920s, and by the 1929–30 season, rates were shown as twelve dollars for a single room with a bath, twenty dollars for a double with a bath, twenty-two dollars for two single rooms with a bath between them and thirty dollars a night for a double and a single with a bath between them. By that time, all rooms had baths available to them, and the "public bath" and "public toilet" facilities shown in the hotel's 1921 plans were no longer extant.

The hotel benefited from not only the hotel company's advertising but also from the fact that in each winter season timetable the railway company would carry a complete list of the hotel company's hotels, a short blurb regarding the facilities, the name of the manager, the number of rooms and the dates of operation for that winter season.

Since the railway and the hotel company, along with longtime passenger train partner Atlantic Coast Line Railroad, which handled FEC trains north of Jacksonville, maintained a joint ticket and reservations office in New

York City at 2 West Forty-fifth Street, it is not difficult to understand the nature of the mutual interest involved, not just at the corporate level but also between individuals working together on a day-to-day basis. Longtime FEC passenger traffic department employee Harold K. North advised me, in a 1984 interview, that a sign behind the counter in that ticket office reminded railroad clerks to ask each patron if he or she would like for the clerk to also make hotel reservations for that person at one of the company's fine hotels in Florida.

With the five terrible events that broke the boom in 1926, hotel reservations, as did passenger train business, declined, and by the 1929–30 season, it had fallen off drastically. The hotel's occupancy for the 1931–32 season barely reached 30 percent, and following that season, according to the *Key West Citizen* in a July 14, 1932 front-page article, the company decided that it would simply close the hotel for the duration of the Depression.

During those years, Key West became the equivalent of a ghost town. FEC passenger train service had been cut from as many as three trains a day in each direction to one, while the Key West yards were nearly devoid of freight cars and dozens of railroad employees were laid off. Numerous Key West businesses closed, and the city administration reached a point at which it literally could not meet payrolls, much less pay

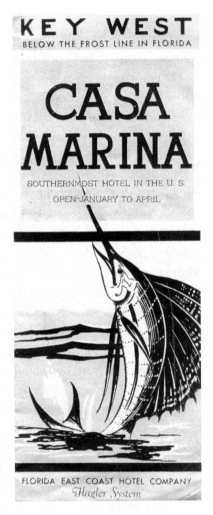

KEY WEST
BELOW THE FROST LINE IN FLORIDA

CASA MARINA

SOUTHERNMOST HOTEL IN THE U. S.
OPEN-JANUARY TO APRIL

FLORIDA EAST COAST HOTEL COMPANY
Flagler System

For the season opening January 1, 1937, the Hotel Company issued this brochure for the Casa, noting that it could be reached by train to Miami, thence via Pan American Airways plane to Key West or via the "reconstructed Overseas Highway," which required "about a four-hour ferry trip from Lower Matecumbe Key." Sadly, the company had, for whatever reason, succumbed to the "restricted clientele" mantra, and the brochure notes that "Casa Marina...is operated on the American plan, and caters to a select clientele," a statement indicating that the hotel no longer accepted guests whom it knew to be of the Jewish faith.

suppliers and fixed obligations. In July 1934, city and county officials asked the state to take over the management and operation of the city.

The governor immediately turned the administrative reins over to the head of the Florida Emergency Relief Administration, and that agency promptly looked to the Federal Works Progress Administration for assistance.

Julius J. Stone Jr. was appointed federal administrator, and as part of his program to rejuvenate and rehabilitate the city, he appealed directly to all solvent employers, requesting their assistance and cooperation in turning the Key West situation around. For the great majority of them, an appeal directly from Washington could not be ignored.

Once again acting in the best interests of Florida, the hotel company not only accepted the challenge but also proceeded to advertise both the Casa Marina and the city itself.

In 1934, the railroad (in receivership since 1931) and the hotel company jointly issued a four-color, four-page, eight-and-a-half- by eleven-inch brochure on high-quality, glossy stock paper titled *Key West/The Island City/ Invites Tourists this Winter*. The back page of the brochure included a large view of the hotel from the water and announced that the hotel would open for the 1934–35 season on December 24.

"Closed for the past three years," the brochure states,

> the Casa Marina will open under a rate schedule beginning at $7.00 per day, each person, American plan. The high standard of service and cuisine for which Flagler System Hotels are distinguished, will be maintained. The opening of the Casa Marina this season adds to the unique appeal of Key West, as a health, yachting and fishing resort, the most modern and comfortable of hotel accommodations.

Casa Marina continued to operate each winter season thereafter until it was sold to the military following the 1939–40 season. However, from the time of the reopening until the sale in 1940, the hotel's management experimented with new and unique methods of increasing business. For example, for each season beginning with 1936–37, the hotel's "formal" opening date was set for mid- to late December, but in order to encourage early arrivals, the hotel announced, immediately below the seasonal dates shown in the descriptive booklets, that they would open and operate "family style from December 1st to opening date."

The Casa Marina

James Ponce, longtime Breakers Hotel employee and that property's historian, as well as a former president of the Palm Beach County Historical Society, explained that the phrase meant that it (the Casa) was doing the same thing as the Breakers was doing in the latter years of the Depression. "To avoid full staffing," Mr. Ponce said, "tables were not assigned in the dining rooms, guests seated themselves and waiters brought out the appropriate meal, with selections being placed on each table and no orders being taken."

The 1937 season began on December 25, but the hotel actually opened on the first for those interested in the family-style approach. It apparently was successful and helped to staunch the decline of the early years of the Depression. The strategy was used until the hotel was sold in 1940.

In that year, with war clouds on the horizon, the U.S. government, as it had done and would do in so many other venues, announced that the Casa Marina was among the hotels that were needed to prepare for the possibility of war. Unlike Miami's Biltmore Hotel, which was converted into a hospital, the Casa became a school and training center, as well as a barracks. After several abortive efforts by a series of postwar owners at reopening the hotel following the war—at one point it also served as a federal jobs training facility—it was taken over by Marriott in 1979 and once again "brought back to life."

After several years of Marriott ownership, the hotel was sold to Waldorf Astoria Resorts. In 2011, managing director Kevin Speidel and his incredibly well-trained staff brought the hotel back to its former glory, and Mr. Speidel told not only his prospective guests but also the people of Key West that "the best is yet to come." Knowing his superb reputation, there is no doubt that the greatest days of the Casa Marina's glory are still ahead.

12

September 2, 1935

As has already been stated several times, the purpose of this book is to tell the whole great and incredible story of the Key West Extension, from the beginning to and through the aftermath of the terrible 1935 hurricane, which destroyed forty miles of right of way, ravaged innumerable buildings and turned the Long Key Fishing Camp into rubble and dozens of buildings in the middle Keys into kindling wood while at the same time causing the deaths of approximately eight hundred people.

While there have been several books dedicated to just the storm (as there have been to just the construction), their credibility may have been, to some extent, compromised by the fact that no research was done at the Bramson Archive.

The full range of facts regarding the hurricane and the FEC's involvement with the storm and its aftermath can now be fully shared with readers primarily because the Bramson Archive houses not only all of the FEC Railway's files regarding the disposition of property following the hurricane but also the file that begins with the telegram asking that a relief train be sent from Miami to pick up the veterans working at Matecumbe and requesting that, as soon as the storm passed, they be brought back to that point.

That file contains the statements of all FEC employees involved in that fateful event and completely belies Ernest Hemingway's breathless and totally fabricated attacks on the railroad in articles he wrote after the storm

September 2, 1935

This page: Pictures of the rescue train on the ground have appeared in numerous publications and books on the 1935 hurricane; hence, it is necessary to show only two here, the first looking north toward Florida Bay showing ten of the eleven derailed cars, with the two boxcars behind the fourth and fifth cars from the front of the train. The second photo shows 4-8-2 447 (the builder's plate of which is currently in the possession of Steve Strunk in Key West) still on the tracks, with the eleven cars strewn about on the left. Both photos were taken on September 4, 1935, by a press photographer.

(very similar to the completely baseless charges of "white slavery" being precipitated during the construction of the railroad in the Keys). In fact, Hemingway had no real or firsthand knowledge of what occurred or how the request for the relief train was handled, which was expeditiously and immediately by the railroad. The fault, if any, should be placed on and with the federal agencies that waited too long to ask that the relief train be made available. However, being Hemingway, he was able to convince readers that much of the fiction he had written regarding the storm and the railroad was truth incarnate.

On September 2, 1935, FEC chief operating officer C.L. Beals sent the following telegraph message to general superintendent A.I. Pooser:

> *Confirming telephone conversation. In order to evacuate F.E.R.A. camp at Matecumbe account approaching storm, arrange operate special train from Miami quick as possible with six coaches two baggage cars and three box cars to Matecumbe to load between four hundred and five hundred F.E.R.A. workers for movement to Hollywood. Party will detrain at Hollywood but will desire to return to Matecumbe some time tomorrow when storm has passed. Officer in charge at Matecumbe is Ray W. Sheldon and he should be contacted for purpose working out details. Conductor should make accurate count of passengers on round trip, which should be promptly reported this office so that bill for collection can be made against F.E.R.A. headquarters Jacksonville.*

Below that is the notation that a copy was being sent to the receivers as information, and below that, on the same page, is a note to Mr. Rahner (Rahner was general passenger agent of the railway) that said:

> *Mr. Rahner—Mr. F.B. Ghent, Director, Florida Emergency Relief Administration, which made telephonic request for this special service this afternoon, and on account of the local representative at Matecumbe not having sufficient funds to pay for the transportation in advance, Mr. Ghent requested that we handle as above outlined, and send bill for collection to him at Jacksonville for payment. I will advise you the number of passengers so that the bill may be prepared by your office.*

September 2, 1935

The next statements in the FEC file are those of F.L. Aitcheson, FEC assistant superintendent; P.L. Gaddis, fifth district superintendent; Buena Vista Yard general yardmaster G.R. Branch; and the crew. Reading those reports gives one a feeling of both sadness and hopelessness as the crew states, one by one, what occurred. Following their statements is the correspondence between Mr. Beals and the receivers relative to issues such as billing for the train (the receivers advised Beals that, due to the fact that the damage to the train was caused by the hurricane, they would not bill the FERA for the trip or the damage), discrepancies in Mr. Ghent's and Mr. Sheldon's statements regarding when they requested the relief train and other material pertinent to the operation of the train.

The file concludes on April 16, 1936, with FEC co-receiver Scott M. Loftin advising J.E. Rankin, chairman of the House Committee on World War Veteran's Legislation, that in response to his (Rankin's) request that FEC employees W.L. Baker (second trick train dispatcher on duty on September 1 and 2) and R.S. Spitz (agent-operator at Islamorada) be sent to Washington to testify, the railroad would be pleased to comply with the request but asked that there be as much advance notice as possible and that they be told approximately when they would be required. Loftin's telegram to Mr. Rankin concludes: "Presume of course these employees will be reimbursed for transportation and time lost."

With that the file ends, for apparently the overwhelming weight of the evidence showed that the delay in requesting the special train had clearly been with the FERA and that the railroad had moved as expeditiously as possible to fulfill the agency's request once it had been received, including Mr. Beal's order, on August 31, that several extra coaches be added to the Havana Special on September 1, "just in case they might be needed."

Writings on and about the storm have ranged from overhyped and ultra dramatic (Hemingway) to "eyewitness," which in many cases referred to those such as former Key West mayor Wilhemina Harvey's description of having ridden the last pre-storm train into Key West. From articles to books, the plethora of tales, stories and accounts of the storm provides the historian, ferreting out the actual and factual from the fanciful, the opportunity to truly understand the viciousness of that hurricane.

With all that has been written, though, two pieces are at hand that seem to combine the best of the drama with what seems to be the complete truth. In

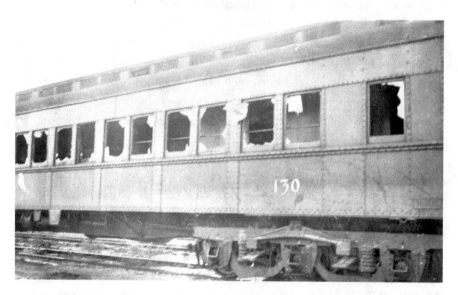

This page: The only known photos of the rescue train after it was brought back to Miami's Buena Vista Yard are owned by the author; they were taken by his dear friend the late Arthur Marsh. When one looks at the damage inflicted upon the steel passenger cars, it is easy to understand how difficult it was for human beings to survive the storm. Note that all of the car's windows were blown out on both the 215 and the 130, while the doors of the 215 and the car to its left have been irreparably damaged.

the July 1956 issue of a magazine named *Men*, a story titled "The Railroad that Blew Away," written by Harold L. Cates as told to Glenn D. Kittler, briefly examines the history of the extension and then goes into a discussion of the storm. While filled with drama, the story notes that "500 veterans and almost as many islanders were killed" and that "Islamorada was wiped out, and so was Tavernier. It took two weeks to gather all the dead and send them off by boat to Miami for burial."

In 1946, reporter and publicist Frank W. Lovering wrote and published "Hurricane Between," and in it he wrote:

> *The advisory at 1:43 PM on Labor Day placed the hurricane 200 miles east of Havana and 180 miles southwest of the Keys. It was still moving west and indications were that only gales would strike the keys.*
>
> *At 4:41 the first warning that the hurricane had swung north-west stated it was advancing toward the Keys. F.B. Ghent, director of Veteran's camp work on the Keys, was in Jacksonville. His assistant, Ray Sheldon, was in Key West and by 4:00 PM Sunday he had reached the camp. Monday morning, deciding it was impractical to wait any longer, he called Miami and asked the Florida East Coast offices how shortly a train could be made up and reach Lower Matecumbe, ninety miles from Buena Vista Yard.*

According to Sheldon, in the course of the investigations, he claimed that he was told that it (making up the train and getting it to Matecumbe) could be done in three hours, but the facts of the investigation proved otherwise.

The request for the train was received by the FEC not later than 2:35 p.m., but preparations had already begun at Buena Vista shortly before 2:00 p.m., as the FEC people had a sense of urgency with the storm approaching the Keys. However, it being a holiday, calling a crew was, in and of itself, no small task, and that, coupled with the need to steam up a locomotive (which would take at least two hours), plus not having a switch engine on duty until 3:00 p.m. to make up the train, was cause for concern. The train, with six coaches, two baggage cars and three boxcars, was further delayed when one of the cars needed air brake repairs, and that held up the train's departure until 4:25 p.m. Sixteen minutes later, the weather bureau in Miami issued a warning notice that the storm had shifted its course.

An incredible image, this view, showing the washed-out trestle that had formerly connected Windley Key (on the left) and Plantation Key (at right), is indicative of the damage that the railroad suffered in the 1935 hurricane.

The train was delayed for ten minutes at the Miami River drawbridge due to boat traffic, and then the conductor and engineer made the decision to turn the locomotive so that, upon reaching Matecumbe and loading the veterans, they could pull out with the engine forward. With the winds rising, a derrick or a signal mast (depending on the account) hooked onto the locomotive, and disentangling it took an hour and twenty minutes. With hell raging across the Keys, the train reached Islamorada at 8:20 p.m.

The horrific blasts of sustained winds roaring across the keys at two hundred miles per hour, coupled with the fearful tidal wave that took the entire train, save the locomotive, off the rails, makes today's student of Florida Keys history, upon seeing the photos showing the deep gouges in the cars after they were brought back to Miami following the storm, wonder how a human being could have survived the storm. In truth, few did.

The remains of Long Key Fishing Camp following the storm. Looking south from just south of the passenger station, it is apparent that there was nothing left to be salvaged.

With the winds increasing by the minute, J.E. Duane, a weather observer on Long Key, dutifully went to work, his observations on the storm being recorded in his journal and then, fortunately for posterity, carried in a story in the *Miami Herald*'s *Tropic Magazine* on Sunday, July 14, 1991, titled "Swept Away."

Without going into a lengthy discussion of the article, the last two paragraphs are so touching that they must be included here:

> *Following the lull* [the eye of the storm] *the hurricane struck again, this time from the south-southwest. The cottage Duane and the others were in was swept out to sea, but in one of those anomalies that mark every hurricane, was somehow re-deposited, intact, back on the shore. Miraculously, all of the inhabitants were still alive.*
>
> *Well over 700 unfortunate souls did not share the same fate. Up and down the keys, wherever the storm had struck, death and devastation were all that was evident.*

Key Largo depot, building 602, following the storm. The bent metal at the left side of the station is all that remains of the semaphore.

Fortunately, I have been in direct contact with two men who, while not in the storm itself, were part of the rescue efforts.

The late Roy Bell, who owned Old Toy Trains, a hobby shop in North Miami, conveyed his experiences in the aftermath of the storm to me in four interviews conducted in June and July 1991. An employee of Standard Oil, Bell was a member of one of the many volunteer rescue teams. "When we got to Long Key," Roy stated, "we were shocked by what we found. And what we found was nothing, not in the sense of a wilderness plain but in the fact that there had been a famous fish [*sic*] camp here and now there was nothing. It was awful."

Bell's descriptions of the eeriness of the scene, the contorted positions of the dead, the physical condition of the injured and the utter desolation are hideously graphic. "It was clear," he said, "that the camp here [on Long Key] was finished, and so was the railroad."

Longtime Miamian Sherman Tobin made the trip down as a teenager, with his father, as Bell had done, hoping to volunteer in an attempt to assist where possible. Mr. Tobin stated to the author that he and his father could not stay for more than two days because the scene was so grisly and heartbreaking.

September 2, 1935

This is the only known photograph of some of the survivors being tended to following the storm. Taken on September 5, 1935, by a press photographer, the condition of the men and the ground they are on tells the whole story. *Courtesy Jerry Groothouse.*

The railroad, after due and proper consideration as mandated by the Interstate Commerce Commission, filed to abandon the tracks south of Florida City, and in due time the petition was granted, with formal abandonment being approved by the commission in 1936. But even with the requisite regulatory and legal delays in obtaining permission to abandon the line, the Key West Extension had, on the night of September 2, 1935, suffered a mortal blow.

Sadly, and surrounded by the pain and suffering that had been caused by the most vicious hurricane, with the lowest barometer readings ever recorded in the western hemisphere, the Key West Extension of the Florida East Coast Railway would, on the very next day, September 3, 1935, surrender to its mortality and pass through the portal of the darkest of nights, into which, at the end of day, all things must go.

Epilogue

"I Can Still Hear the Whistle of Train Number 75 Blowing for the Matecumbe Crossing!"

M any—if not most—books dealing with history generally end with these words, or something similar: "And that is the end of the story." This tells the reader that this is it, the story of the historical event is over and nothing else is going to happen from this point forward.

The thing is, when it comes to *this* history, this incredible tale of the greatest railroad story ever told, it doesn't simply end. For while the history part of the story may have had its climax with the terrible hurricane of September 2, 1935 (or depending on one's point of view, with the opening of the Overseas Highway in 1938), the fact of the matter is that, whether in the minds and memories of those few still alive who got to see the railroad in operation or to ride the trains or those to whom has fallen the duty and obligation to see to it that the memory of Henry Flagler and what he and his successors did for Florida is never forgotten, the story of the Key West Extension, the greatest railroad engineering and construction feat in U.S. (and—possibly—world) history will never truly end.

It appears that the earliest efforts to preserve the memories of the extension and those who worked on it began in 1952, when, according to an article in the *Miami Herald* dated Sunday, January 20, 1952, and headlined "Reunion to Honor Men Who Built Keys Railroad," "A group of Miamians, as significant in Florida's history as the Pilgrim fathers were to New England, will gather in Key West this week for a reunion on the 40th anniversary of an epochal achievement."

The first (and, it appears, the last) reunion of the construction veterans was held at the Casa Marina in Key West on Wednesday, January 23, 1952. Attendees included, *from left*: Carlton Corliss, J. Ernest Cotton and Henry H. (Hy) Hyman. *Courtesy Monroe County Public Library.*

The Miami contingent, as stated in the article, was headed by H.H. Hyman, who, at the time, was southern division manager for Florida Power and Light Company. The group planned to meet for lunch at the formerly Flagler System–owned Casa Marina Hotel in Key West on Wednesday, January 23, to celebrate the anniversary.

The article mentions several individuals whose names have never before been shown on documents or in previous books and who were unable to attend the gathering, including Calvin Oak, who at the time the article was written was president of Riverside Bank in Miami and who had been administrative assistant for the entire project, and E.R. "Doc" Lowe, of Tavernier, who ran the dispensary (medical facility) for construction workers at Marathon.

Among the Miami-area attendees were construction department engineers and employees Hyman, James Dunaway, W.A. Glass and J. Ernest Cotton, as well as Key Wester Ed Strunk Jr., founder of Strunk Lumber Company in the island city. According to his grandson, Steve Strunk of Key West, Strunk was hired in Miami to work on the extension at the office of Roddey Burdine, of department store fame, and then went to work for the railroad in 1914 at the age of sixteen. He worked full time in the Marathon office for several of the engineers for two years.

Carlton Corliss came down from Washington for the reunion and was so moved by it and by seeing so many of his longtime friends and comrades that he vowed to at least attempt to form some sort of informal organization composed of those who had the shared experience of working on the extension. In October

1954, Corliss published the first of two issues of what he called the *Extensioneer*, which, as he wrote, was not meant to be "a weekly, nor a monthly, nor even a quarterly but it will appear occasionally as the spirit moves and when there is something to write about." Although only two issues were published using the thankfully long-gone mimeograph process, the information contained therein is priceless, and the first issue (volume 1/number 1) contains the names of all who attended the reunion held at the Casa Marina on January 22, 1952.

Although, sadly, every one of the men and women named is deceased, the memories of them and the incredible work they did will live on for as long as there is a Florida. Although they have left us, what remains are the memories, the artifacts and the memorabilia.

While it is true that there are precious few large physical artifacts remaining of the railroad's presence in the Keys (the three mile-post markers, one at MP 492 on Big Pine Key, thirty miles north of Key West; one at a restaurant in Key Largo; and one at a private home in Matecumbe, and the bollards that are still in place on the docks at Key West, along with the buildings on Pigeon Key, may be all that exists), there are smaller and equally important pieces in public and private collections, including the only known bridge builder's plate removed intact from the Seven Mile Bridge; the American Railway Express Company's Key West, Florida wax sealer; the only known Henry Flagler Seven Mile Bridge pier paperweight still in good condition, a numbered group that he commissioned and had made in the exact proportionate height and weight for its size and gave as gifts following the opening of the extension, all in the Bramson Archive, along with the badges worn by members of the Over-the-Sea Railroad Celebration Committee and souvenir plates and silver pieces that commemorate the twenty-three years, seven months and eleven days of operation, which may be all that is known to have survived in other than paper or photographic form.

Yet thankfully, it appears that thousands of photographs, negatives, postcards and railroad-related correspondence, booklets, brochures and timetables have lived on to tell the incredible story, and those pieces, whether in Key West, the Keys or other locations, are the mainstay of what some might think of as the fanciful, if it were not completely factual, history of Henry Flagler's railroad that went to sea.

In addition to the Bramson Archive (the largest collection of FEC Railway and Florida transportation memorabilia in the world, containing

In October 1954, Carlton Corliss published the first issue of the *Extensioneer*, meant to serve as an occasional newsletter to help the veterans of the construction remain in touch. Unhappily, only two issues were published.

approximately three thousand oversea railway images [photographs, negatives and postcards], as well as several thousand FEC passenger and employee timetables, booklets, brochures, maps and correspondence on and dealing with the extension), there are a good few museums or historic trust sites along the former route of the railway that have worked to preserve the great and incredible past so that it is available for future generations to learn not only what Mr. Flagler and his colleagues did in building the railroad but also how the railroad operated for the more than twenty-three years preceding the 1935 hurricane and what it meant to the Keys in general and Key West in particular.

The largest of the museums is in the Custom House at Key West, which is owned and managed by the Key West Art and Historical Society under the direction of Claudia Pennington with the incredible cooperation of the board of directors, of which the ebullient David Harrison Wright is president. Their centennial of the railroad's arrival in Key West exhibit is the linchpin for all other events in regard to the 100th anniversary.

The Pigeon Key Foundation, even though, for the moment, accessible only by boat from Knight's Key, has, for some years, preserved the history of the railroad, particularly as it affected Pigeon Key.

The Matecumbe Historical Trust has, since its founding, worked diligently to preserve the historic heritage of the Keys, and now, after many years of ardent and dedicated devotion to the task is preparing to, in April 2012, open the Irving R. Eyster Museum of Florida Keys History.

The Monroe County Public Library in Key West has, almost since its founding, worked tirelessly to catalogue oversea railway items, first through the efforts of Helen "Mike" Purdy and then thanks to her successor in the Florida collection, Tom Hambright. The library is a fine repository of photographs and other Keys memorabilia.

Numerous individuals have also worked hard to preserve the heritage of the Keys, including Dr. Dan Gallagher, Ed Swift, Steve Strunk, Joan and the late Wright Langley, Jonathan Nelson, Calvin Winter and, of course, those no longer with us, from Carlton Corliss to Arthur Marsh—the list of those who have helped is lengthy, including so many of our friends and colleagues in the Florida East Coast Railway Society.

As some readers may already know, and with the proper deference being shown to those named above, I am often called upon, as company historian, to give talks on the history of the FEC. In so doing, when I am in the Keys and talk about the history of the railroad below Homestead, I eventually reach the point, in the presentation, of describing the terrible Labor Day 1935 hurricane, and the reaction of a few individuals to my comment that "over 800 people were killed" is related above. But what is not related above is one of the strangest, if not eeriest, stories that anyone has ever heard relating not just to an American railroad but also specifically to the years of operation of the Florida East Coast Railway in the Keys.

To the best of my knowledge, although no one has yet tried to claim (and this with some of the truly "doozy" claims that are made in regard to Keys history) that he or she has seen the ghosts of those who died in any of the hurricanes, there is one statement that recurs almost every time I tell the great story of the railroad's history at some venue in the Florida Keys.

When I conclude the segment on the FEC's operations in the Keys and before I go on to the years of the receivership and the Depression as the lead-in to the introduction of the new, streamlined trains in 1939, I have noticed, no few times, that one person (and, on occasion, two people) will, very hesitatingly, start to raise his or her hand(s), and since the first time that happened, I know exactly what is coming, for it has now happened a good few times.

None of the construction veterans are now alive, and sadly, few who rode the train to or from Key West remain. Fortunately, the physical memorabilia and artifacts will always and ever serve to remind the world of the great feat. Mile post 275/247 is just one example of the memorials that still exist, ensuring that the greatest railroad story ever told will never be forgotten. *Courtesy Mark L. Poormon.*

The person wishing to say something will, usually, stand up very slowly and then will say, in a haltingly slow manner, with pauses between words, "Seth…I know this…sounds crazy…[the words falter]…but…but on those dark and cloudy nights, when the wind is still and there is no moon…[and then a lengthy pause]…I can still hear the whistle of train number 75 blowing for the Matecumbe crossing."

The room is absolutely silent, and for some moments nobody speaks or, for that matter, moves, and although my audience does not know it, I alone among the attendees, know what is coming next.

One person, and then another and, sometimes, even a third person will say, "I've heard it, too, but I was afraid." And somebody else will then respond, "I didn't think anybody else heard it, and I thought that if I said something people would think that I was crazy."

The truth is, none of those people are crazy. If anything, they are both lucid and blessed, for the sound of train number 75, the southbound Havana Special thundering across the islands, viaducts and bridges, with its whistle blowing for the several crossings, will echo across the Keys for as long as there are people who recognize the importance of the railroad that went to sea, what it meant to the people it served and how it served as the lifeline of Keys commerce for the twenty-three-plus years of its existence.

May they never stop hearing that glorious sound.

ABOUT THE AUTHOR

S eth Bramson is one of only two people in the country who bears the official title of company historian with an American railroad, and his book *Speedway to Sunshine: The Story of the Florida East Coast Railway* is the official history of that famous line.

He is a co-founder of the FEC Railway Society, and his collection of FEC Railway and Florida transportation memorabilia is the largest in the world. It is larger than the state museum's collection and larger than the Flagler Museum's collection, and he is the senior collector of that material in America. May 2012 will begin his fifty-sixth year of collecting.

The founder and current president of the Miami Memorabilia Collectors Club, Bramson's collection of Miami memorabilia and Floridiana is the largest in private hands in the country, and he is a member of almost every historical organization in South Florida.

America's single most published Florida history book author, this book is his twenty-first. Sixteen of his books memorialize the histories of the villages, towns, cities, counties, people and businesses of the South Florida Gold

Coast, and the other five deal with the FEC and the railway/steamship/ hotel system of the famous Henry Plant, who did for the west coast of Florida what Mr. Flagler did for the east coast.

Bramson is adjunct professor of history at Barry University, Florida International University and Nova Southeastern University's Lifelong Learning Institute and has been married to his beloved Myrna for more than thirty-five years.

Printed in the USA
CPSIA information can be obtained
at www.ICGtesting.com
LVHW080825011123
762556LV00006B/137